My
Picture
Thesaurus

Helping your child

- Using a thesaurus requires several different skills, from identifying letters and words to recognizing the order of letters in the alphabet. This picture thesaurus has been designed to help your child develop these key abilities.

- To help your child get the most benefit from this picture thesaurus, these suggestions may be useful:

- To find a particular word in the thesaurus, point to the alphabet strip on each page and encourage your child to look for the initial letter of the word they need. Ask them to find the page(s) with that letter highlighted.

- Once on the page, your child may need support to find the word they are looking for. Help them to use the alphabet strip to work out where the second, third, etc. letters in the word fall in the alphabet, then look through the word lists to locate it.

- Use the gold stars stickers as incentives and rewards for your child learning some of the words or spellings.

This edition published by Parragon Books Ltd in 2017

Parragon Books Ltd
Chartist House
15–17 Trim Street
Bath BA1 1HA, UK
www.parragon.com

Copyright © Parragon Books Ltd 2017

Written by Sue Graves and Emily Stead
Illustrated by Simon Abbott
Designed by Cloud King Creative

ISBN 978-1-4748-6984-3

Printed in China

My Picture Thesaurus

PaRRagon

Bath · New York · Cologne · Melbourne · Delhi
Hong Kong · Shenzhen · Singapore

Introduction

What is a thesaurus?

A **thesaurus** is similar to a dictionary. But instead of just giving you the meaning of the word you have looked up, as a dictionary does, a thesaurus gives you a list of other words with similar meanings (*synonyms*). Sometimes a thesaurus also gives you words with opposite meanings (*antonyms*).

A thesaurus is a very useful book. It can increase your written and spoken vocabulary and help you use more interesting words when you write!

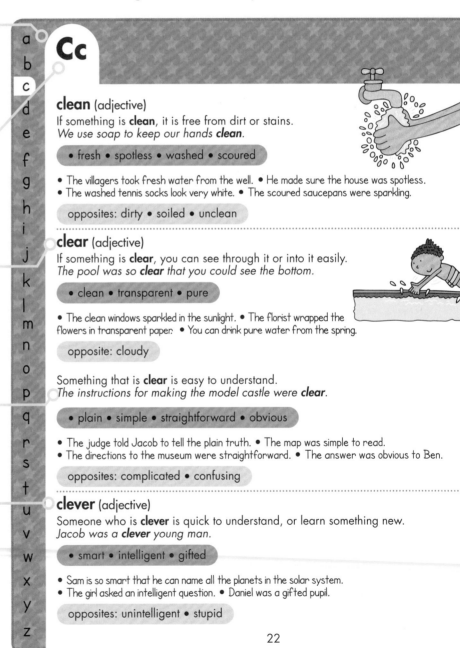

alphabet band

For each letter of the alphabet, there is a different coloured band across the top of the page.

alphabet letter

The letters inside the tab tell you that all the words on this page begin with the letter **c**.

headword

The headword is the main word that you look up to find synonyms for it. The headwords appear in alphabetical order.

example sentence

This shows how you can use the headword in a sentence.

part of speech

This tells you what kind of word the headword is: noun, verb, adjective, adverb or preposition.

a b **c** d e f g h i j k l m n o p q r s t u v w x y z

Cc

clean (adjective)
If something is **clean**, it is free from dirt or stains.
*We use soap to keep our hands **clean**.*

- fresh • spotless • washed • scoured

- The villagers took fresh water from the well. • He made sure the house was spotless.
- The washed tennis socks look very white. • The scoured saucepans were sparkling.

opposites: dirty • soiled • unclean

clear (adjective)
If something is **clear**, you can see through it or into it easily.
*The pool was so **clear** that you could see the bottom.*

- clean • transparent • pure

- The clean windows sparkled in the sunlight. • The florist wrapped the flowers in transparent paper. • You can drink pure water from the spring.

opposite: cloudy

Something that is **clear** is easy to understand.
*The instructions for making the model castle were **clear**.*

- plain • simple • straightforward • obvious

- The judge told Jacob to tell the plain truth. • The map was simple to read.
- The directions to the museum were straightforward. • The answer was obvious to Ben.

opposites: complicated • confusing

clever (adjective)
Someone who is **clever** is quick to understand, or learn something new.
*Jacob was a **clever** young man.*

- smart • intelligent • gifted

- Sam is so smart that he can name all the planets in the solar system.
- The girl asked an intelligent question. • Daniel was a gifted pupil.

opposites: unintelligent • stupid

22

How to use this thesaurus

Words are listed alphabetically in a thesaurus, just like they are in a dictionary. The word you look up first of all is the headword. After the headword, you can find out what part of speech the word is and what it means. You will also find a sentence showing you how to use the word.

Next, you will find a list of synonyms. These are followed by sentences that show how you might use the synonyms in your writing. If the headword has antonyms (opposites), these are listed last.

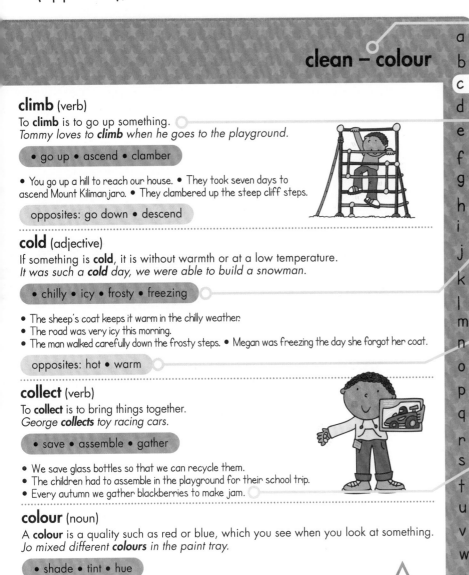

clean – colour

a b **c** d e f g h i j k l m n o p q r s t u v w x y z

climb (verb)
To **climb** is to go up something.
*Tommy loves to **climb** when he goes to the playground.*

• go up • ascend • clamber

• You go up a hill to reach our house. • They took seven days to ascend Mount Kilimanjaro. • They clambered up the steep cliff steps.

opposites: go down • descend

cold (adjective)
If something is **cold**, it is without warmth or at a low temperature.
*It was such a **cold** day, we were able to build a snowman.*

• chilly • icy • frosty • freezing

• The sheep's coat keeps it warm in the chilly weather.
• The road was very icy this morning.
• The man walked carefully down the frosty steps. • Megan was freezing the day she forgot her coat.

opposites: hot • warm

collect (verb)
To **collect** is to bring things together.
*George **collects** toy racing cars.*

• save • assemble • gather

• We save glass bottles so that we can recycle them.
• The children had to assemble in the playground for their school trip.
• Every autumn we gather blackberries to make jam.

colour (noun)
A **colour** is a quality such as red or blue, which you see when you look at something.
*Jo mixed different **colours** in the paint tray.*

• shade • tint • hue

• Her jumper was a pretty shade of blue.
• The painter added a red tint to the white paint.
• The model had a dress in every hue.

23

header words
The words at the top of the pages show you the first and last headwords that appear on the page(s).

definition
This gives you the meaning of the headword.

synonyms
The synonyms have similar meanings to the headwords.

opposite
This means the opposite of the headword. Not all headwords have an exact opposite.

example sentences
These show you how you can use the synonyms and help you to understand their exact meaning.

gold stars
Add a gold star sticker when you've learned some of the words.

Aa

able (adjective)

Being **able** means having the power or ability to do something.
*The magician was **able** to produce a rabbit out of a hat.*

> • capable • skilful

* She was capable of writing neatly when she tried.
* Jenny was a skilful basketball player.

> opposites: incapable • unable

about (adverb)

About means almost or close to. • *Jim had **about** ten more maths questions to finish.*

> • almost • approximately • nearly • roughly

* It was almost time for dinner. • The bus was approximately five minutes late.
* There were nearly 50 bales of hay in the barn. • Roughly 200 children attended school today.

above (preposition)

Something that is **above** is higher up.
*The helicopter flew **above** the clouds.*

> • over • on top of • upon

* The walkers climbed over the hill to the other side.
* The window cleaner stood on top of the ladder.
* Mum put seven candles upon the birthday cake.

> opposites: below • under

absent (adjective)

If you are **absent** from something, you are away from it.
*Andy was **absent** from school because he had chicken pox.*

> • away • gone • missing

* The Jones family was away for the holidays. • There were lots of cakes, but suddenly they were gone! • Grandma was worried because her pet cat was missing.

> opposites: present • here

accident (noun)

An **accident** is something bad that happens by chance.
*Liam had an **accident** in his PE lesson.*

> • disaster • crash • collision

- It was a disaster when the school burned down.
- Two big tankers were involved in the crash.
- The collision took place on an icy road.

active (adjective)

An **active** person or animal moves around a lot.
*Luke keeps **active** by playing tennis.*

> • lively • energetic • vigorous

- The lively children ran around the playground.
- The circus acrobats were very energetic.
- The boys played a vigorous game of football.

actor (noun)

An **actor** is someone who performs in a film or a play.
*The **actor** stood in the middle of the stage.*

> • player • performer • star

- The three players bowed in front of the audience.
- The street performer made everyone laugh.
- The star of the film wore a beautiful dress.

add (verb)

You **add** numbers together to find their total.
*You can use a calculator to **add** a list of numbers.*

> • count • total

- My little brother can count up to 100.
- The shopkeeper had to total the day's takings.

> opposite: subtract

Aa

admire (verb)

To **admire** means to like and respect something or someone.
*The people went to the museum to **admire** the paintings.*

> • adore • praise • worship

• "I adore pop music," said Donna.
• The teacher praised the children's good work.
• She worshipped her older sister and her friends.

admit (verb)

To **admit** is to accept that something is true.
*The thief wouldn't **admit** that he had stolen the money.*

> • accept • own up • confess • acknowledge

• Ben cannot accept that he is no longer in the football team.
• He owned up to breaking the window. • I told my brother to confess the truth.
• She acknowledged that the mess was her fault.

> opposite: deny

adult (adjective)

Adult means grown-up. • *Joe approached the problem in an **adult** manner.*

> • fully grown • grown-up • mature

• Most cats are fully grown by the time they are two years old.
• The young swimmers were accompanied by two grown-up lifeguards.
• The prefects behave in a mature way.

afraid (adjective)

If you are **afraid**, you are scared or frightened.
*The boy was very **afraid** of spiders.*

> • scared • fearful • frightened • terrified

• Our kitten is scared of loud noises. • The fearful knight
ran away from the battle. • The puppy was frightened by
the big dog. • The old man was terrified of ghosts.

> opposites: confident • unafraid

agree (verb)

If you **agree** with someone, you think the same as that person.
*Everyone **agreed** that the new building was ugly!*

> • get along • concur • accept • side with

• Ben gets along well with his brother. • The teacher concurred that the maths test was hard.
• The doctor accepted that his patient was sick. • Lucy always sides with Mark during an argument.

> opposite: disagree

alert (adjective)

If you are **alert**, you are ready for action.
*The security guard was **alert** as he opened the door.*

> • attentive • observant • watchful • sharp

• Jack is attentive and always listens carefully to his teacher.
• The burglar was spotted by an observant police officer.
• The soldiers were watchful in case the enemy attacked.
• The sharp girl spotted the missing jewel.

amazing (adjective)

Amazing means something that causes great surprise or wonder.
*My grandma is an **amazing** lady.*

> • astonishing • surprising • staggering

• The boy ate an astonishing number of doughnuts. • Our teacher told us a surprising fact.
• We received some staggering news.

amusing (adjective)

Something that is **amusing** is funny and makes people laugh.
*The circus clowns were really **amusing**.*

> • enjoyable • funny • hilarious

• Everyone had an enjoyable time at the show.
• The girls watched a funny cartoon on TV.
• Mark told a hilarious story about his dog.

> opposites: boring • dull

Aa

angry (adjective)

Angry means cross or annoyed.
*Dad was **angry** when the dog ate his lunch.*

> • annoyed • cross • displeased • furious

• We were annoyed because the bus was late. • Grandad gets cross when he loses his glasses. • The teacher was displeased with the noisy class. • Mary was furious when her brother took her sweets.

annoy (verb)

If you **annoy** people, you irritate them. • *Joe liked to **annoy** his big sister.*

> • bother • irritate • pester • tease

• "Don't bother me now," said Mum, reading her book. • The rash on my arm began to irritate me. • The twins always pester their mum when they go shopping. • I tease my best friend about her purple hair!

> opposite: please

answer (verb)

When you **answer**, you say or write something to someone who asks a question.
*"How old are you?" the reporter asked. "Eight," **answered** Katie.*

> • reply • respond • retort

• The thief replied quickly to the police officer's question. • The waiter responded to our complaint about the food. • "That's such an awful headline!" retorted the journalist.

appear (verb)

If something **appears**, it moves to a place where you can see it.
*The ghost suddenly **appeared** in the doorway.*

> • come into view • come to light • loom • turn up

• The ship came into view over the horizon.
• The missing documents came to light after a search.
• A sinister figure loomed out of the fog.
• Michael was sure his missing trainers would turn up.

> opposite: disappear

argue (verb)

If you **argue** with someone, you do not agree with that person.
*The girls **argued** about whose turn it was.*

> • bicker • disagree • quarrel • squabble

• The brothers bicker about which football team is the best.
• My friend and I disagree over silly things. • When people quarrel, they often shout
at each other. • Martha and Emily squabbled over the remote control for the TV.

> opposite: agree

arrange (verb)

If you **arrange** something, you plan it and put it into practice.
*I'm going to **arrange** a surprise party for my friend's birthday.*

> • plan • prepare • organize

• It took a long time to plan our safari trip. • The hotel staff prepared the conference room.
• He organized a meeting between the parents and the teachers.

ask (verb)

You **ask** a question in order to find out the answer.
*I **asked** how much it cost to gift-wrap the present.*

> • request • query • interrogate • enquire

• The dentist requested that I come back in six months. • The farmer queried what the vet said.
• The police officer interrogated the suspect. • Molly enquired whether I was feeling better.

> opposites: answer • reply

awful (adjective)

Awful means very bad or unpleasant. • *Rosie had an **awful** cough.*

> • bad • horrible • unpleasant • ugly

• Oscar's bad behaviour upset his mum. • Josh was horrible to his sister yesterday.
• The ice cream had an unpleasant taste.
• Litter in the street looks really ugly.

> opposites: good • nice

Bb

baby (noun)

A **baby** is a young child or animal.
The **baby** was only six months old.

> • newborn • child • infant • babe

- The woman cradled her newborn boy.
- The young child loved to draw and paint.
- Meg was the smallest infant in the nursery.
- Emily's daughter is still just a babe in arms.

> opposite: adult

bad (adjective)

Bad means ill-behaved or morally wrong.
*The **bad** dog always barked when he saw the postman.*

> • naughty • wicked • evil

- Our naughty cat got stuck in the apple tree. • "What a wicked thing to say!" said Mum.
- The witch cast an evil spell.

> opposite: good

If food is **bad**, it is not fit for you to eat.
*Tim ate a **bad** apple and had stomach ache.*

> • rotten • mouldy • spoiled • sour

- The rotten pears are scattered on the ground.
- Mum put the mouldy cheese in the rubbish bin.
- The food was spoiled because of the heat. • No one could drink the sour milk.

bake (verb)

To **bake** is to cook something in an oven.
*My grandpa likes to **bake** a cake every Friday.*

> • cook • heat • roast

- My dad wears an apron when he cooks.
- The chef heated the apple pie until it was warm.
- If you roast meat slowly it will be tender to eat.

band (noun)

A **band** is a number of people who play music together.
*I decided to form a **band** with my friend.*

> • group • orchestra • ensemble

- The pop group has made a new album.
- There are over 100 musicians in the orchestra.
- An ensemble played music during the wedding.

A **band** is a thin strip of rubber, metal or
other material. • *Tom wore a red **band** on his wrist.*

> • ring • strap • strip

- Beth was proud of her diamond ring. • The traveller fastened the strap around his suitcase.
- The nurse put a strip of bandage over the wound.

bare (adjective)

If something is **bare**, it is not covered up.
*The **bare** trees had lost all their leaves.*

> • naked • uncovered • nude

- Babies are naked when they are born.
- I left the graze on my knee uncovered to heal in the fresh air.
- Some beaches allow nude sunbathing.

> opposites: clothed • covered

beautiful (adjective)

If something is **beautiful**, it is very attractive.
*The peacock is a **beautiful** bird.*

> • attractive • charming • fine • lovely

- The garden looks most attractive in spring.
- The little boy had a charming smile.
- The shoes were made of fine leather.
- There are many lovely flowers in the park.

> opposites: ugly • unattractive

a b c d e f g h i j k l m n o p q r s t u v w x y z

Bb

behave (verb)

To **behave** means to act in a certain way.
*Our puppy **behaves** well if you praise him.*

> • act • conduct • react

- The guide asked the children to act sensibly in the museum.
- You should conduct yourself quietly in a church.
- The teacher did not react when the class was being silly.

> opposite: misbehave

bend (verb)

If you **bend** something, you make it more curved.
*David tried to **bend** and touch his toes.*

> • twist • curve • turn

- Jane twisted her long hair into a big knot. • The road curves to the left.
- The man turned the key in the lock.

> opposite: straighten

better (adjective)

Better means higher quailty, or more pleasing or effective.
*The tomato soup tasted much **better** once it was seasoned.*

> • preferable • improved • superior

- Travelling by train is preferable to catching a bus.
- My netball skills are much improved after practising all year.
- Isla's painting was superior to mine.

To feel **better** means that you are in good health, after feeling ill.
*Ellen was feeling **better** after having mumps.*

> • recovered • stronger • fitter • well

- He recovered quickly after the operation.
- Beth was a lot stronger and able to get out of bed.
- The athletes are fitter after training hard.
- Now that Sarah is well she can start dancing again.

big (adjective)

Something that is **big** is large.
*The giant was **bigger** than a house.*

> • large • vast • immense • enormous • huge

- We take a large suitcase with us on holiday.
- The Sahara desert is vast. • The king lived in an immense castle.
- A blue whale is an enormous animal. • My dad has huge hands.

> opposites: little • small • tiny

boast (verb)

To **boast** means to talk proudly about yourself, your things, or something you have done. • *"I am the best wizard in the whole world," **boasted** Mr Magic.*

> • brag • gloat • show off • crow

- Mrs Brown was always bragging about her smart son. • The rich man gloated about his big car.
- Sam showed off his medal after the race. • Ella crowed with delight when she won first prize.

boring (adjective)

Boring means dull and not very interesting.
*Everyone thought the chemistry lesson was **boring**.*

> • dull • dreary • uninteresting • tedious

- The party was dull because there were no games. • Dad's office job is dreary most of the time.
- Emily thought the book was uninteresting. • The passengers found the long journey tedious.

> opposite: interesting

bottom (noun)

The **bottom** of something is the very lowest part of it.
*The shipwreck lay at the **bottom** of the ocean.*

> • base • foot • bed

- The climbers camped at the base of the mountain. • Tom called me from the foot of the stairs. • The bed of the river was covered with stones.

> opposite: top

a b c d e f g h i j k l m n o p q r s t u v w x y z

bottom (noun)

You sit on your **bottom**.
*Owen slipped on the banana skin and fell on his **bottom**.*

> • backside • rear • bum (slang) • behind

- My backside hurt after sitting on the hard bench.
- The rider slapped the horse's rear to make it trot.
- She fell over on the ice and hurt her bum. • The baby sat on the floor on his behind.

brave (adjective)

If you are **brave**, you are not afraid to do something.
*The **brave** boy climbed to the top of the climbing wall.*

> • bold • fearless • daring • plucky

- The bold princess fought the dragon. • Fearless Tom dived from the high diving board.
- Anna was daring enough to jump off the rock. • Mum was very plucky to tackle the burglar.

> opposites: afraid • scared • timid

break (verb)

If you **break** something, you damage it, or separate it into pieces.
*If you kick a ball against a window, it will usually **break**.*

> • crack • shatter • fracture • snap

- The storm was so strong that it cracked the ship's mast.
- The falling brick shattered the window.
- If you fracture your leg it will be put in a cast.
- The boy hit the ball so hard that he snapped his bat.

> opposites: fix • mend • repair

break (noun)

A **break** is a short rest or a change in something.
*We got out of the car for a short **break**.*

> • rest • pause • intermission • gap

- The athlete needed a rest after the long race. • There was a short pause in the music.
- We chatted during the intermission in the play. • The fox squeezed through a gap in the fence.

bright (adjective)

Something that is **bright** is shiny and gives off light.
*The stars in the night sky were very **bright**.*

> • shiny • dazzling • brilliant • glaring

- I found a shiny coin in the street today.
- The stars were dazzling in the night sky.
- The brilliant diamond sparkled in the light.
- Sunglasses protect your eyes from glaring sunlight.

> opposites: dim • dull

A **bright** person is smart and quick to learn. • *Penny was a very **bright** student.*

> • brainy • smart • intelligent • clever

- Bob was so brainy that he passed all his tests.
- The smart boy thought of a good plan.
- The intelligent woman liked doing difficult crossword puzzles.
- The clever dog could open the door with his teeth.

bring (verb)

If you **bring** something, you carry it with you.
*If you **bring** back your library book, you can choose another.*

> • carry • fetch

- The porter carried her suitcase onto the train.
- Dad told the dog to fetch his slippers.

build (verb)

If you **build** something you make it or put it together.
*We decided to **build** the wall out of bricks.*

> • make • assemble • construct

- Dad is going to make a tree house for us.
- Flora tried to assemble the bookcase by following the instructions.
- The builders constructed the new shed very quickly.

> opposites: demolish • destroy • knock down

a b c d e f g h i j k l m n o p q r s t u v w x y z

building (noun)

A **building** is a structure with a roof and walls, such as a house or factory.
*The old run-down **building** was going to be turned into offices.*

> • construction • structure • dwelling

- This church is an ancient construction. • Our city library is a magnificent structure.
- Four families shared the dwelling.

burn (verb)

If something **burns**, it catches fire and gives off flames.
*When we make a bonfire we usually **burn** wood.*

> • blaze • flame • flare

- The fires blazed across the forest.
- A match will flame briefly and then go out.
- When Mum fanned the fire, the flames flared up.

bury (verb)

If you **bury** something you place it under the ground.
*Our puppy likes to **bury** his bones in the back garden.*

> • conceal • cover • hide

- The pirates wanted to conceal their treasure in the cave.
- The desert sand covered the ruins of the ancient city.
- Squirrels sometimes hide their acorns under tree roots.

> opposites: dig up • uncover

busy (adjective)

If you are **busy**, you have lots to do.
*Fridays were always **busy** at work.*

> • active • occupied • bustling

- The children spent an active day swimming and climbing.
- My brother was occupied all day in his bedroom.
- The headteacher is always bustling around her office.

> opposites: idle • inactive

Cc

call (verb)

If you **call**, you shout out for someone.
*The teacher **called** our names one at a time.*

● announce ● cry ● yell ● shout

- The referee announced the names of the winning teams.
- "Come back here!" cried the dog trainer.
- The coach yelled to the players on the field.
- Tom was told not to shout in class.

calm (adjective)

Calm means quiet and not worried or excited.
*The sea was **calm** in the bay.*

● quiet ● still ● peaceful ● serene

- The children played a quiet game of cards.
- You could not hear a sound in the still night.
- Grandpa enjoyed the peaceful surroundings of the park.
- The old soldier had a serene expression.

care (verb)

If you **care** about something or someone, you think a lot about that person or thing.
*"I really do **care** about you!" Jack's worried mum said to him.*

● mind ● be concerned ● worry

- "I don't mind if it rains," said the gardener.
- The pilot was concerned that his plane was damaged.
- We were worried when William arrived home late.

carry (verb)

When you **carry** something, you hold it and move it with you.
*April had to **carry** a pile of books to the school library.*

● take ● move ● transport

- We must take the rubbish to the dump.
- The removal company moved the furniture into our new house.
- Lorries transport goods all over the country.

a b c d e f g h i j k l m n o p q r s t u v w x y z

Cc

catch (verb)

If you **catch** something, you take hold of it in your hands.
The coach kicked the ball for Tom to catch.

> • arrest • capture • trap • grab

• The police officer set off to arrest the thief. • The zookeeper tried to capture the escaped parrot. • A spider traps flies in its web. • Ali's mum told us not to grab the sweets.

> opposites: drop • free • miss

certain (adjective)

To be **certain** is to be sure about something.
*Josh was running so fast, he was **certain** he would win.*

> • confident • satisfied • positive • sure

• Dan has worked hard and is confident that he will pass the test. • The baker was satisfied that he had baked enough cakes. • Luke was positive that he had handed in his homework. • The driver was sure that the bus would arrive on time.

> opposites: doubtful • uncertain • unsure

change (verb)

When something **changes** it becomes different.
*I **change** into my uniform before I go to school.*

> • alter • transform • modify • vary

• Mum is going to alter my new dress because it's too big. • The decorator transformed her bedroom into a princess's palace. • The general had to modify his battle plans. • Dad likes to vary his route to work each week.

chase (verb)

To **chase** is to run after someone or something.
*Dogs like to **chase** cats.*

> • run after • hunt • pursue • track

• The hungry leopard ran after the herd of gazelle. • Our cat goes out to hunt for food at night. • The shopkeeper pursued the man who stole his money. • The guide tracked the elephants by following their footprints.

a b c d e f g h i j k l m n o p q r s t u v w x y z

cheap (adjective)

If something is **cheap**, it does not cost much money.
*The bananas in the supermarket were very **cheap**.*

- reasonable • inexpensive • reduced • affordable

• Mum says we can buy the computer game if it's a reasonable price.
• Jasmine bought an inexpensive dress in the sale. • The shop had some reduced items after Christmas. • The builder was selling some affordable new houses.

opposites: costly • expensive

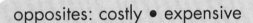

check (verb)

When you **check** something you make sure it is right.
*The sailor went to **check** that the ropes were fastened tightly.*

- examine • inspect • test

• He examined the used car very carefully. • The conductor inspected our train tickets.
• Dan tested the bath to see how warm it was.

child (noun)

A **child** is a young boy or girl.
*Every **child** should hold hands with someone when crossing the road.*

- baby • infant • toddler • kid • youngster

• Our baby likes to sleep in his car seat. • The infant was learning to crawl.
• She takes her toddler to nursery every morning. • Kids eat for free at the restaurant in town.
• The youngster beat much older opponents in the chess tournament.

opposites: adult • grown-up

choose (verb)

To **choose** is to decide which thing you want from a larger number. • *Adam went to **choose** a new shirt for the party.*

- select • pick • elect

• The captain was asked to select players for her team. • We picked our favourite toys from the catalogue. • Every few years people elect a new prime minister.

Cc

clean (adjective)

If something is **clean**, it is free from dirt or stains.
*We use soap to keep our hands **clean**.*

- fresh • spotless • washed • scoured

- The villagers took fresh water from the well. • He made sure the house was spotless.
- The washed tennis socks look very white. • The scoured saucepans were sparkling.

opposites: dirty • soiled • unclean

clear (adjective)

If something is **clear**, you can see through it or into it easily.
*The pool was so **clear** that you could see the bottom.*

- clean • transparent • pure

- The clean windows sparkled in the sunlight. • The florist wrapped the flowers in transparent paper. • You can drink pure water from the spring.

opposite: cloudy

Something that is **clear** is easy to understand.
*The instructions for making the model castle were **clear**.*

- plain • simple • straightforward • obvious

- The judge told Jacob to tell the plain truth. • The map was simple to read.
- The directions to the museum were straightforward. • The answer was obvious to Ben.

opposites: complicated • confusing

clever (adjective)

Someone who is **clever** is quick to understand, or learn something new.
*Jacob was a **clever** young man.*

- smart • intelligent • gifted

- Sam is so smart that he can name all the planets in the solar system.
- The girl asked an intelligent question. • Daniel was a gifted pupil.

opposites: unintelligent • stupid

22

climb (verb)

To **climb** is to go up something.
*Tommy loves to **climb** when he goes to the playground.*

> • go up • ascend • clamber

• You go up a hill to reach our house. • They took seven days to ascend Mount Kilimanjaro. • They clambered up the steep cliff steps.

> opposites: go down • descend

cold (adjective)

If something is **cold**, it is without warmth or at a low temperature.
*It was such a **cold** day, we were able to build a snowman.*

> • chilly • icy • frosty • freezing

• The sheep's coat keeps it warm in the chilly weather.
• The road was very icy this morning.
• The man walked carefully down the frosty steps. • Megan was freezing the day she forgot her coat.

> opposites: hot • warm

collect (verb)

To **collect** is to bring things together.
*George **collects** toy racing cars.*

> • save • assemble • gather

• We save glass bottles so that we can recycle them.
• The children had to assemble in the playground for their school trip.
• Every autumn we gather blackberries to make jam.

colour (noun)

A **colour** is a quality such as red or blue, which you see when you look at something.
*Jo mixed different **colours** in the paint tray.*

> • shade • tint • hue

• Her jumper was a pretty shade of blue.
• The painter added a red tint to the white paint.
• The model had a dress in every hue.

Cc

come (verb)

To **come** is to move towards someone or something.
*Rachel asked everyone to **come** to her party.*

> • arrive • approach • reach

- Our friends are due to arrive at 2 o'clock.
- We approached our classroom through the main school gate.
- The passenger reached the station just in time to catch the train.

contain (verb)

To **contain** is to have or hold something inside.
*This box **contains** two delicious cupcakes.*

> • hold • consist • include • comprise

- The pouch holds up to 30 coloured marbles.
- A stew usually consists of meat and vegetables.
- The book includes 100 stickers.
- Our school library comprises thousands of books.

cook (verb)

When you **cook**, you prepare food by heating it.
*I like to help my dad **cook** dinner.*

> • make • heat • prepare

- My brother makes lots of different kinds of soup.
- It's easy to heat a pizza in an oven.
- The chef prepared a banquet for 500 people.

correct (adjective)

If something is **correct**, it is right. • *The cashier gave me the **correct** change.*

> • right • accurate • true • precise

- I gave the right answer to the teacher's question.
- The boy gave an accurate description of the accident.
- The man took off the mask to reveal his true identity.
- My watch always tells the precise time.

> opposites: incorrect • wrong

a
b
c
d
e
f
g
h
i
j
k
l
m
n
o
p
q
r
s
t
u
v
w
x
y
z

cosy (adjective)

Cosy means warm and snug.
*Javinder was **snug** inside his sleeping bag.*

> • comfortable • snug • warm

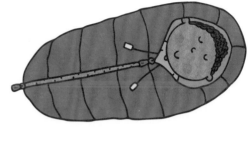

- The sofa is a comfortable place to relax.
- My woolly jumper keeps me snug in the winter.
- We kept warm sitting in front of the fire.

count (verb)

When you **count**, you use numbers to work out how many things there are.
*I **counted** five ducks swimming on the pond.*

> • add • total • calculate

- The waiter added up our bill.
- The mechanic totalled the cost of the car repairs.
- Joe calculated the number of days until his birthday.

creature (noun)

A **creature** is an animal. • **Creatures** *called dinosaurs roamed the earth millions of years ago.*

> • animal • beast

- There are lots of animals in the city zoo.
- We spotted the tracks of a wild beast.

crisp (adjective)

If something is **crisp**, it is hard and dry.
*The biscuits were very **crisp** because we had baked them for too long.*

> • hard • crunchy • firm

- The hard toffee was difficult to chew.
- My rabbit loves to eat crunchy carrots.
- This racehorse gallops faster on firm ground.

> opposite: soft

Cc

cross (adjective)

If you are **cross**, you are angry about something.
*The twin looked **cross** in her school photograph.*

> • annoyed • angry • irritated • grumpy

- The passengers were annoyed because their train was late.
- The old man was angry with the rowdy children.
- Our noisy neighbours irritated Mum.
- Grandad is grumpy first thing in the morning.

cruel (adjective)

Someone who is **cruel** is unkind to other people or to animals.
The **cruel** boys kicked the old dog.

> • brutal • heartless • vicious • ruthless

- The gang launched a brutal attack. • The heartless thief stole the family's laptop.
- The footballer made a vicious tackle. • Napoleon was ruthless in battle.

> opposites: gentle • kind

crush (verb)

To **crush** something is to squash it by pressing hard.
*We **crushed** the cans, then put them in the recycling bin.*

> • flatten • squash • compress • mash

- The dog flattened the flowers with his huge paws. • Luke had to squash his clothes into a small suitcase. • A huge machine compresses the old cars into scrap metal.
- You can mash boiled potatoes with milk and butter.

cut (verb)

To **cut** something is to divide it or open it with scissors or a knife.
*The mayor **cut** the ribbon and declared the new library open.*

> • carve • chop • clip • slice • trim

- Grandpa always carves the Sunday roast.
- Megan chopped off her ponytail.
- Dad likes to clip the hedge to make it neat.
- The chef sliced the vegetables with a huge knife. • I trim my hair when it gets too long.

Dd

damage (verb)

To **damage** something is to harm it. • *Sam **damaged** his toy when he dropped it.*

> • destroy • devastate • ruin • wreck

• The flood destroyed the old bridge. • The strong winds will devastate the wheat crop.
• Sam ruined his bicycle when he crashed into a wall. • The huge waves wrecked the tiny rowing boat.

> opposites: fix • mend • repair

danger (noun)

A **danger** is something that might cause harm or injury.
*The ship was in **danger** because of the stormy seas.*

> • risk • threat • peril • hazard

• The man took a risk when he dived into the icy lake.
• The weather forecast says there is a threat of rain tomorrow.
• The explorers found themselves in peril when they went off course.
• In the winter, ice can be a hazard on the roads.

dark (adjective)

Dark means there is little or no light. • *I used my torch to find my way in the **dark**.*

> • dim • gloomy • murky • shadowy

• It was dim inside the cinema. • The prison cell was gloomy
and cold. • It was a murky morning because of the thick fog.
• John thought he saw a shadowy figure by the wall.

> opposites: bright • light

decide (verb)

When you **decide**, you choose. • *She **decided** to buy the red roses.*

> • choose • determine • resolve • conclude

• I always choose vanilla ice cream for dessert.
• "Your behaviour today will determine whether you can go
to the party," said Dad. • Mum resolved to go for a run three
times a week. • The doctor concluded that her patient should go to hospital.

Dd

delicious (adjective)

Something that is **delicious** tastes very good.
*We ate a **delicious** pizza in the Italian restaurant.*

> • appetizing • tasty • scrumptious • yummy

- They found Chinese food quite appetizing.
- The meat from the barbecue was very tasty.
- "Your homemade pudding tastes scrumptious!" said Naomi.
- The children thought that Ben's birthday cake was yummy.

> opposites: horrible • unpleasant • revolting

destroy (verb)

To **destroy** means to spoil or to ruin. • *The bulldozer will **destroy** the factory building.*

> • demolish • knock down • ruin • wreck

• My little brother loves to demolish towers of bricks. • The workers had to knock down the old house. • "You will ruin your new shoes in the rain," warned Dad. • The vandals wrecked the flowerbeds in the park.

> opposites: build • create

different (adjective)

Something that is **different** is not the same.
*We each chose a **different** flavoured milkshake.*

> • opposite • contrasting • assorted

- Meg and her mum have opposite views about music.
- Black and white are contrasting colours. • We ate assorted snacks at the party.

dig (verb)

To **dig** is to break up the ground with a spade or a shovel.
*Gemma had to **dig** the vegetable patch before planting new crops.*

> • burrow • excavate • scoop • tunnel

• Moles like to burrow under the ground. • The students had to excavate the old Roman temple.
• You scoop soil out of the ground when you plant bulbs. • The prisoners managed to tunnel underground and escape.

dirty (adjective)

Something that is **dirty** is covered or marked with dirt.
*Kate was **dirty** from head to toe after the hike.*

> • filthy • grimy • grubby • muddy

- The rags were filthy after I used them to clean the car.
- These grimy windows have not been washed for years.
- The children were grubby after playing in the yard.
- It was fun jumping in the muddy puddle!

> opposite: clean

disaster (noun)

A **disaster** is an event that causes great loss or suffering.
*The famine was the worst **disaster** in many years.*

> • accident • catastrophe • calamity

- Tom broke his leg in a skating accident. • The damage from the flood was a catastrophe for the islanders. • It was a calamity when I lost my passport on holiday.

discover (verb)

To **discover** is to find something or to find out about it.
*Patrick's map helped him **discover** lots of interesting places nearby.*

> • find • detect • unearth • uncover

- It took ages for Daniel to find his trainers.
- The machine detected a fault in the system.
- The dog unearthed the bone he had buried.
- The historian hoped to uncover some prehistoric remains.

do (verb)

If you **do** something, you go ahead with it or finish it.
*My brother likes to **do** his exercises every morning.*

> • carry out • perform • achieve • complete

- The servants carry out lots of duties in the palace. • Our dog can perform funny tricks. • Max achieved a record time in the swimming pool.
- I completed the marathon in just under four hours.

doubt (verb)

If you **doubt**, you are not sure about something or someone.
*Kelly began to **doubt** that she would get to school on time.*

> • suspect • mistrust • hesitate • question

- The judge suspected the witness's account.
- I mistrusted my brother after he lied to me. • The driver hesitated about which road to take.
- The scientists questioned the researcher's findings.

> opposites: believe • trust

draw (verb)

When you **draw**, you use a pencil or crayon to make a mark.
*This artist likes to **draw** space rockets.*

> • sketch • trace • doodle

- The art class tried to sketch the flowers on the table. • Ben traced the design on to his book. • My little sister has doodled on my English textbook.

If something **draws** you, you want to move closer to it.
*The film star always **draws** a huge crowd of fans.*

> • attract • bring • entice • pull in

- Colourful plants in the garden attract butterflies.
- The reduced prices bring lots of customers to the shop.
- Mum enticed the kitten down from the tree with a bowl of milk.
- The opening night of the show pulled in a huge audience.

dry (adjective)

If something is **dry**, it is free from liquid, or not wet.
*The desert was a **dry** place, as it never rained there.*

> • arid • parched • thirsty

- Only a few trees grew on the arid land.
- The fields were parched because it had not rained for months.
- Ted was thirsty after playing tennis in the hot sunshine.

> opposite: wet

Ee

eager (adjective)

If you are **eager**, you really want to do or have something.
*Katy was **eager** to show off her best ballet moves.*

> • enthusiastic • impatient • keen

- The audience was very enthusiastic about the new band.
- The passengers were impatient to board the plane.
- Clare was keen to practise her ice-skating.

easy (adjective)

Something that is **easy** does not require much effort to achieve it.
*We thought the maths test was **easy**.*

> • clear • simple • straightforward • plain

- A set of clear instructions is included with the model plane. • The chemistry experiment was simple once the teacher had explained it. • The directions to our new house are very straightforward. • The car manual was written in plain language.

> opposites: difficult • hard

eat (verb)

When you **eat**, you chew food and then swallow it.
*My favourite thing to **eat** is spaghetti!*

> • chew • consume • munch • swallow

- Mum told Fred to chew his food properly. • Our dogs consume a lot of food each day.
- Horses like to munch hay. • After you have chewed your food, you swallow it.

empty (adjective)

If something is **empty**, it has nothing or no one in it.
*The box was **empty** because we had eaten all the chocolates.*

> • bare • vacant • unoccupied • hollow

- The floor was bare with no carpet or rugs on it. • The house was vacant after the students moved out. • The old mansion has been unoccupied for many years. • A family of owls lives inside the hollow tree trunk.

> opposite: full

a b c d e f g h i j k l m n o p q r s t u v w x y z

Ee

end (noun)

The **end** of something is the last part of it.
*The audience clapped at the **end** of the concert.*

> • ending • finish • conclusion

- The novel had an exciting ending.
- There was a thrilling finish to this year's marathon.
- The meeting was finally brought to a conclusion.

> opposites: beginning • start

end (verb)

If something **ends**, it stops or finishes. • *Our school term **ends** in the middle of July.*

> • finish • conclude • stop • cease

• Matthew finished his homework before going out to play. • The concert concluded with a piano solo. • The rain finally stopped after lunch. • The fighting ceased when the police arrived.

> opposites: begin • start

enjoy (verb)

If you **enjoy** something, you really like doing it.
*Tim and Kelly **enjoy** watching television.*

> • appreciate • like • love

• My mum appreciates a home-cooked meal. • We like to eat outdoors in the summer.
• The twins love visiting the local farm.

> opposites: detest • hate • loathe

enormous (adjective)

Enormous means very big. • *Elephants are **enormous** creatures.*

> • gigantic • huge • giant • massive

• A gigantic wave swept over the ship. • A huge rock fell from the cliff. • The explorers found some giant footprints in the snow. • Mount Everest is a massive mountain.

> opposites: little • small • tiny

enough (adjective)

If you have **enough** of something, you have as much as you need.
*Dad bought **enough** food to last the whole week.*

> • ample • adequate • sufficient

• The greengrocer had an ample supply of apples.
• There was adequate food for all the children at the school picnic.
• There is a sufficient supply of water on the island.

> opposites: inadequate • insufficient

even (adjective)

If something is **even**, it is flat and smooth. • *The concrete floor was perfectly **even.***

> • flat • smooth • level

• The paper was folded into a flat shape. • The girl had smooth, shiny hair.
• A level pathway led to the metal gate.

> opposites: bumpy • rough

If two things are **even**, it means they are the same.
*Jack and Luke had **even** amounts of popcorn.*

> • the same • level • equal

• Mary and Beth wore the same dresses. • The paintings on the wall were level with each other.
• The twins were given equal amounts of money for their birthday.

> opposite: different

evil (adjective)

Evil means bad or wicked. • *The **evil** witch casts spells on her enemies.*

> • bad • wicked • hateful • wrong

• "Any bad behaviour and the trip will be cancelled," said the teacher.
• The burglar was wicked to steal from the old lady. • The cruel man was hateful to his cat. • It is wrong to steal from other people.

> opposite: good

excellent (adjective)

Excellent means very good.
*Jack got **excellent** grades in his report.*

> • outstanding • superb • wonderful

• Emma trained hard to become an outstanding rider. • Lucy played a superb game of tennis.
• Everyone had a wonderful time at my birthday party.

excited (adjective)

Excited means happy and lively.
*Pete is so **excited** – it's his birthday today!*

> • lively • thrilled • boisterous

• The playground was full of lively children. • The boy was thrilled by the magician's amazing tricks. • Sam and Michael were so boisterous that they broke a chair.

> opposite: bored

explain (verb)

To **explain** is to make something easy to understand.
*The instructor **explained** how to use the new running machine.*

> • clarify • make clear • demonstrate

• The manager clarified what to do when the fire alarm rings.
• Mr Jones made clear that he expected us to behave well in class.
• The chef demonstrated how to make perfect pastry.

extraordinary (adjective)

Something that is **extraordinary** is very unusual.
*Fred's aunt is wearing an **extraordinary** hat.*

> • amazing • bizarre • strange • unusual

• Jim did an amazing dive into the pool.
• Todd got a bizarre present from his grandfather. • Our local novelty store sells strange things.
• The unusual design for the new school building won first prize.

> opposites: ordinary • usual

Ff

fair (adjective)

Something **fair** is reasonable and right. • *A referee has to be **fair** to both teams.*

> • just • equal • right • proper

• The prisoner received a just punishment for his crime.
• Mum gave us equal amounts of ice cream. • Everyone agreed that Jack was the right choice for team captain. • The jury tried to make proper decisions about the court case.

> opposite: unfair

fall (verb)

To **fall** is to drop downwards. • *Gravity makes apples **fall** from trees.*

> • drop • descend • dive • plunge

• The parachutist started to drop down to the ground.
• The lift descends to the next floor in the store.
• The children wanted to dive into the deep end of the pool.
• Kingfishers plunge to grab fish from the water.

> opposite: rise

famous (adjective)

Someone who is **famous** is well known to lots of people. *The **famous** pop star performed for her fans.*

> • well-known • eminent • celebrated

• I spotted a well-known film star in the street. • The eminent scientist won a Nobel prize. • The celebrated artist held an exhibition.

fantastic (adjective)

Fantastic means made up or fanciful. • *Simon wrote a **fantastic** story about aliens.*

> • far-fetched • extraordinary • incredible • amazing

• Leah gave a far-fetched excuse not to go to school.
• The actors wear some extraordinary costumes in the film.
• My uncle told us about his incredible adventures.
• Unicorns are amazing creatures.

Ff

fast (adjective)

Someone or something that is **fast** can move quickly.
*The **fast** cars sped around the racetrack.*

> • quick • speedy • rapid • swift

• I go for a quick walk every morning. • Owen has a speedy new scooter. • The rapid train reaches London in less than two hours. • The gazelle is a swift and graceful animal.

> opposite: slow

fat (adjective)

Fat means big and rounded.
*We only feed our rabbits grass and hay, so they won't get **fat**.*

> • plump • chubby • overweight • tubby

• Dad roasted a plump chicken for dinner. • Carl had a chubby pig as a pet. • Eating too much unhealthy food may make you overweight. • Ellie's teddy bear is fluffy and tubby.

> opposites: slim • thin

fear (noun)

You feel **fear** when you think something bad is about to happen to you.
*The knight had a real **fear** of dragons!*

> • fright • terror • dread • alarm

• Ben gave his sister a fright when he jumped out of the cupboard.
• The scary film filled the audience with terror.
• I was full of dread at the start of the exam.
• The guard cried out in alarm when the fire started.

feel (verb)

If you **feel** something, you touch it to find out what it's like.
*If you touched a snake it would **feel** warm and dry.*

> • touch • stroke • pet

• You must not touch the displays in the museum.
• My rabbit loves it when I stroke her.
• Kittens purr when you pet them.

fierce (adjective)

Fierce means angry and dangerous. • *The **fierce** lion let out a loud roar.*

> • dangerous • ferocious • savage • vicious

• The hippopotamus is a large and dangerous animal. • The two teams got into a ferocious argument. • The castle suffered a savage attack. • The guard dog is vicious if you get too close to it.

> opposite: gentle

fight (verb)

If you **fight** someone you try to hurt that person.
*The boys always **fight** over the same toys.*

> • battle • struggle • brawl • grapple

• Centuries ago, knights went into battle on horseback. • The two girls struggled over the new tablet. • The rival teams were brawling on the pitch. • The two warriors grappled with each other.

fill (verb)

If you **fill** something, you make it full. • *We will easily **fill** this basket with plums.*

> • cram • load • pack • stuff

• It is rude to cram your mouth with food. • The men loaded the furniture into the removal van. • The dentist packed lots of appointments into her busy day. • Mum will stuff the toy horse with a special filling.

> opposites: clear out • empty

find (verb)

When you **find** someone or something, you come across what you have been looking for. • *Amy searched high and low to **find** her diary.*

> • notice • spot • trace • discover

• I noticed the lost kitten under a bush. • A stolen car was spotted at the end of the street. • My aunt has been trying to trace her long-lost brother for years. • The walkers had to discover the way home for themselves.

> opposite: lose

a b c d e f g h i j k l m n o p q r s t u v w x y z

Ff

finish (verb)

When you **finish** something, you come to the end of it.
*Peter was keen to **finish** his book.*

> • end • conclude • stop

• The film ended at 10 p.m. • The show concluded with a big chorus.
• Grandma told us to stop being so noisy.

> opposites: begin • start

fix (verb)

If you **fix** something, you make it work again.
*Tom had to **fix** the chain on his bike.*

> • repair • mend • patch

• The garage will repair my damaged car.
• Mum mended the broken desk lamp.
• Grandpa patched the broken window in his greenhouse.

> opposite: break

fly (verb)

To **fly** is to move through the air.
*When the weather is windy, we love to **fly** kites.*

> • soar • glide • swoop • float

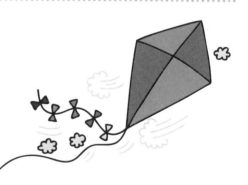

• Eagles soar high into the sky. • The plane started to
glide towards the runway. • The gull swooped to catch a fish.
• A feather will float slowly down to the ground.

follow (verb)

If you **follow**, you move along behind a person or thing.
*The kids **follow** their teacher into the classroom.*

> • pursue • chase • trail • track

• The police officer pursued the burglar. • Our dog likes to chase cats.
• The private detective trailed the main suspect.
• The ranger tracked the animals across the plain.

38

forget (verb)

If you **forget** something, you do not remember it.
*Do not **forget** to feed your pet every day.*

> • ignore • omit • overlook

- Sarah tried to ignore the bully in her class.
- The airline omitted some names from the passenger list.
- The teacher said he would overlook Joe's bad behaviour this time.

> opposite: remember

free (adjective)

If something is **free,** you do not have to pay money for it.
*The tickets to the open-air concert were **free**.*

> • complimentary • on the house

- We were given complimentary tickets to the theatre.
- The new restaurant owner gave his first customers a meal on the house.

If something is **free**, it is not being used.
*The seats in the front row were all **free**.*

> • available • vacant • unoccupied

- The next available flight from Bristol was at 2 p.m.
- I asked the hotel manager if he had any vacant rooms for the night.
- We couldn't find any unoccupied seats on the train.

> opposites: in use • occupied • taken

friend (noun)

A **friend** is someone you know and like.
*Alex and Charlie are best **friends**.*

> • pal • companion • ally

- Tom missed his pals when he moved house. • Mrs Brown's dog was a good companion. • France and America were Britain's allies in World War II.

> opposite: enemy

Ff

frighten (verb)

If you **frighten** someone, you scare that person.
*The older boy tried to **frighten** his cousin.*

> • alarm • scare • startle • terrify

• I felt alarmed when the balloon burst suddenly. • The spooky film scared the audience. • If you startle a horse it may rear up.
• Big snakes terrify many people.

> opposites: calm • reassure

frown (verb)

If you **frown**, you make an angry face at something or someone.
*The actor **frowned** when the audience talked during the play.*

> • glare • scowl • glower • grimace

• Mum glared at me when I said something I shouldn't have. • The goalkeeper scowled when the other team scored. • The general glowered at his soldiers. • I grimaced in pain when I fell over.

> opposites: grin • smile

funny (adjective)

Something that is **funny** makes you laugh.
*Lily giggled as she read the **funny** story.*

> • amusing • comical • hilarious • entertaining

• There are some amusing cartoons in this magazine. • The clown made everyone laugh with his comical dance. • Everyone enjoyed the hilarious movie. • We went to see an entertaining show.

> opposites: sad • serious

Something that is **funny** is a little surprising or out of the ordinary.
*Sam had a **funny** feeling that someone was following him.*

> • odd • peculiar • strange • unusual

• The art teacher liked to wear odd clothes. • The hot chocolate tasted really peculiar.
• Jasmine saw a strange car in the street. • Mum wore an unusual hat to my sister's wedding.

Gg

gentle (adjective)

Someone who is **gentle** is soft and kind. • *The mother cat was so **gentle** with her kittens.*

> • soft • mild • tender

• The announcer spoke in a soft voice. • There was a mild breeze at the coast. • Hannah gave her dad a tender smile.

> opposites: harsh • rough

get (verb)

Get can mean to receive or have something. • *Jo hopes to **get** a new car next year.*

> • acquire • obtain • earn • receive

• Alison acquired her grandmother's jewels. • Everyone wants to obtain the latest computer games.
• I am going to earn a lot of money from babysitting. • Jenny received a new book from her aunt.

> opposite: lose

give (verb)

To **give** means to let someone have something.
*Bea made a birthday card to **give** to her dad.*

> • grant • present • donate • provide

• The fairy granted the princess three wishes. • The referee presented the trophy to the captain. • We were asked to donate money to the charity. • The teacher provided us with the answers.

> opposites: receive • take

glad (adjective)

If you are **glad**, you are pleased and happy. • *I'm **glad** that my cousin is coming to stay.*

> • pleased • delighted • happy • joyful

• Dan was pleased with his new skateboard. • Grandma was delighted to see all her grandchildren. • The children had a happy time at the beach.
• Ellie wished all her friends a very joyful Christmas.

> opposites: sad • unhappy

a b c d e f g h i j k l m n o p q r s t u v w x y z

Gg

go (verb)

To **go** is to move towards or away from something.
*It is safe for vehicles to **go** when the lights turn to green.*

> • depart • leave • set off

- The train will depart from platform six.
- We must leave the house at three o'clock.
- My parents set off early for the beach.

> opposites: remain • stay

go (noun)

To give something a **go** means to try it.
*Last year I gave skateboarding a **go**.*

> • try • effort • attempt

- Dad persuaded me to give fractions a try.
- We made an effort to play our new board game.
- The archer hit the bullseye on the first attempt.

good (adjective)

If you are **good** you behave well. • ***Good** children always share.*

> • well-behaved • polite • virtuous • obedient

- The class was well behaved on the school trip.
- Peter was a polite boy. • King Frederick was a virtuous ruler.
- Laura has a very obedient dog.

> opposite: naughty

If something is **good**, it is of the best quality.
*We watched a **good** film last night.*

> • excellent • super • first class • splendid

- The pianist was an excellent musician. • My uncle cooked a super meal.
- The TV show was first class. • Michael made a splendid model of a monster.

> opposite: bad

grab (verb)

If you **grab** something, you take it quickly.
*Holly **grabbed** her pencil, ready to start work.*

> • seize • snatch • pluck

- The captain tried to seize the stowaways.
- It is rude to snatch when someone hands you something.
- The sailor leaned over the side to pluck the girl from the water.

grand (adjective)

Something that is **grand** seems impressive and important.
*The King and Queen looked very **grand**.*

> • dignified • impressive • glorious • majestic

- Ben's dad looked dignified in his new suit. • The visitors thought the palace was very impressive. • The ramblers had a glorious day out in the country. • We admired the majestic scenery.

> opposites: humble • modest

great (adjective)

If something is **great**, it can mean it is large in size or in number.
*There was a **great** steeple on top of the church.*

> • big • immense • enormous • vast

- The big cruise ship sailed into the harbour. • The researcher had an immense knowledge of his subject. • The young vet had an enormous love of animals. • A vast crowd gathered to see the parade.

> opposites: little • small • tiny

greedy (adjective)

You are **greedy** if you have or want more than is fair, or more than you need.
*The **greedy** girl ate too much cheese.*

> • gluttonous • voracious • selfish

- The gluttonous pig never stopped eating.
- The voracious queen wanted more land than anyone else.
- The selfish player would not pass the ball to her team mates.

a b c d e f g h i j k l m n o p q r s t u v w x y z

Gg

grow (verb)

When something **grows** it gets bigger.
Sunflowers often grow taller than people.

> • develop • increase • swell

- Small seeds develop into leafy plants.
- The fund for the new school quickly increased.
- The balloon swelled as I blew into it.

> opposite: shrink

group (noun)

A **group** is a collection of people, animals or things.
The United Kingdom is made up of a small group of countries.

> • collection • set • bunch • band

- I have over 50 dolls in my collection. • We sorted the crayons into sets.
- Dave bought his mum a bunch of flowers. • The pop band had four members.

guess (verb)

If you **guess** something, you think it is right, but you are not sure.
The man guessed the answer correctly.

> • think • estimate • suspect

- I think I might get a new surfboard for my birthday.
- The carpenter estimated that it would take a week to make the cabinet.
- The police suspect that at least two people carried out the robbery.

guide (verb)

If you **guide** someone, you show that person how to do or find something.
There was no one to guide the explorers through the jungle.

> • direct • lead • accompany • usher

- The police officer directed the traffic. • The firefighter led the patients out of the burning hospital. • My older sister accompanied us to the sports centre. • The officials ushered the athletes into the sports village.

handsome (adjective)

A **handsome** person or object is good-looking.
*The **handsome** prince came riding into the kingdom.*

- attractive • fine • good-looking

• The bride and groom made an attractive couple. • The pyjamas were fine quality. • Mrs Allen was proud of her good-looking son.

opposite: ugly • unattractive

happen (verb)

If something **happens**, it occurs or takes place.
*Accidents sometimes **happen** if you take risks.*

- take place • occur • arise

• Jamie's party took place at the bowling alley. • Your birthday occurs on the same date each year.
• Arguments often arise between the rival football teams.

happy (adjective)

If you are **happy**, you feel pleased or content.
*Toby felt **happy** when he won a gold medal.*

- blissful • contented • delighted • thrilled

• The children had a blissful holiday at the lake. • Ben was a very contented baby.
• I was delighted to get an invitation to the opening of the new art gallery.
• Josh was thrilled to get a part in the school play.

opposites: sad • unhappy

hard (adjective)

If something is **hard**, it is very difficult.
*The students did not like the **hard** maths test.*

- tough • difficult • demanding

• It was tough work planting the new trees. • It was difficult to find a cure for the disease. • The teacher gave us some demanding homework.

opposite: easy

a b c d e f g h i j k l m n o p q r s t u v w x y z

Hh

hard (adjective)

A **hard** object is firm and solid.
*The stone seat was **hard** and uncomfortable.*

> • rigid • firm • unyielding

- The fragile statue was packed in a rigid container.
- You have to put bathroom scales on a firm surface.
- It was impossible to push open the unyielding door.

> opposite: soft

harm (verb)

To **harm** means to hurt someone or something.
*Alex was careful not to **harm** the butterfly.*

> • damage • hurt • injure • ruin

- Very strong winds may damage buildings.
- When the horse jumped the fence it hurt its leg.
- I injured my leg when I fell off the swing.
- Spilling milk onto a table will ruin the wood.

> opposites: benefit • help

hate (verb)

If you **hate** something, you do not like it at all.
*We **hate** eating Brussels sprouts.*

> • despise • detest • dislike • loathe

- We all despise bullies at school.
- Some people detest spiders.
- I dislike doing my homework.
- Kelly loathes tidying her bedroom.

> opposites: like • love

have (verb)

If you **have** something, it belongs to you.
*Dan and Jessie **have** a rabbit called Floppy.*

> • own • possess • hold

- Susie owns five teddy bears.
- Dad possessed hundreds of books.
- The winning team holds the sports trophy for a year.

heal (verb)

To **heal** is to get better or to make something or someone better.
*The x-ray showed that my wrist needed time to **heal**.*

> • cure • soothe • mend

• The ointment cured the itchy rash. • Honey and lemon helped soothe my sore throat. • Dad mended a hole in my favourite skirt.

> opposites: harm • hurt

heavy (adjective)

Something that is **heavy** weighs a lot.
*The elephant was far too **heavy** for the scales.*

> • hefty • massive • weighty

• The old man could not lift the hefty box. • The movers tried to carry the massive chest.
• A St Bernard is a weighty dog.

> opposite: light

help (verb)

If you **help** someone, you assist that person.
*My brother **helped** me make a lemon meringue pie.*

> • aid • assist • support

• Some people use a cane to aid walking. • We offered to assist the new teacher. • The social worker supports families who are in trouble.

> opposite: hinder

hide (verb)

To **hide** means to keep out of sight. • *Eva **hides** her secret diary in a shoebox.*

> • secrete • conceal • cover up

• The smugglers decided to secrete the barrels in a cave. • The fox concealed itself under the bush. • The accountant tried to cover up his mistakes.

> opposites: display • show

Hh

high (adjective)

If something is **high**, it is up above other things.
*The hot-air balloon flew over the trees, **high** above the ground.*

• lofty • tall • towering

• The giant looked down from his lofty height. • Bea is tall for her age. • In New York there are many towering skyscrapers.

opposites: low • short

hit (verb)

To **hit** something means to strike it.
*Ben can **hit** balls from all over the court.*

• strike • punch • thump • batter

• Lightning can strike twice in the same place. • The footballer punched the air when he scored.
• Rabbits thump their hind legs on the ground when they sense danger.
• The rain battered the window panes.

hold (verb)

To **hold** something means to have it in your hands or arms.
*Remember to always **hold** hands when crossing busy roads.*

• carry • cradle • grasp • clasp

• The foreman asked us to carry the bricks. • The nurse cradled the newborn baby carefully. • Dad grasped the ladder while Mum climbed into the attic. • The toddler clasped his favourite teddy bear.

opposites: let go • release

horrible (adjective)

If something is **horrible**, it is very unpleasant. • *Ella had a **horrible** cold.*

• dreadful • awful • unpleasant • nasty

• The weather today was dreadful. • My mum had an awful day at work. • The burnt food tasted really unpleasant. • She said some nasty things about her new neighbour.

opposites: lovely • wonderful

hot (adjective)

If something is **hot**, it is very warm. • *"Careful, that pan is **hot**!" warned Dad.*

* scorching • sweltering • scalding

* The sun was scorching so I put on my hat. • Emma was sweltering in her woolly sweater.
* The soup was scalding, so we waited for it to cool down.

opposite: cold

hungry (adjective)

When you are **hungry**, you need to eat food.
*Alice was **hungry** after her dance class.*

* ravenous • famished • starving

* Dad was ravenous, so he bought a sandwich. • The walkers were famished after their long hike.
* I missed breakfast, so I was starving by lunchtime.

opposite: full

hurry (verb)

To **hurry** means to move or act quickly. • *Luke had to **hurry** to catch the train.*

* rush • hasten • dash

* We had to rush to school because we were late.
* The injured athlete did special exercises to hasten his recovery.
* She dashed inside as it started to rain.

opposites: dally • dawdle

hurt (verb)

To **hurt** means to damage someone or something.
*Beth **hurt** her finger when she trapped it in the door.*

* bruise • harm • injure • wound

* I bruised my leg when I tripped over the log.
* Kelly tried not to harm the little mouse.
* If you fall off a horse you might injure yourself.
* Many soldiers returned home wounded after battle.

Ii

idea (noun)

An **idea** is a thought or plan in your mind.
*Willow had a great **idea** for a story.*

> • concept • plan • theory • suggestion

• The garden design was the architect's concept.
• The prisoners made a plan to escape.
• The scientist was sure his theory was right.
• Our captain's suggestion about the game was the best.

ideal (adjective)

Something that is **ideal** is just right in every way.
*This spot is the **ideal** place for our picnic.*

> • perfect • excellent • faultless • model

• She found the perfect shoes to match her outfit. • "That apple pie was excellent!" said Joe.
• The launch of the space rocket was faultless. • My teacher says that I am a model student.

> opposites: imperfect • wrong

ignore (verb)

To **ignore** something means to pay no attention to it.
*Mum decided to **ignore** the cat's bad behaviour.*

> • disregard • overlook • turn a blind eye

• "I cannot disregard your past offences," said the judge. • The director overlooked all
the actor's good work. • The nurse turned a blind eye to the patient's complaints.

ill (adjective)

When you are **ill**, you don't feel well. • *Alice is **ill** in bed with chickenpox.*

> • sick • unwell • queasy • ailing

• I visited my sick cousin in hospital.
• George felt unwell after such a big meal.
• She felt queasy when she travelled on the boat.
• My ailing grandma has to go to the doctor.

> opposites: healthy • well

important (adjective)

If something is **important**, it is of great value.
*My grandad is an **important** person in my life.*

> • high-ranking • key • leading • urgent

• A colonel is a high-ranking officer in the army. • Jasmine is a key player in the basketball team. • The young actor had a leading role in the play. • Mr King got an urgent letter from his lawyer.

> opposite: unimportant

impossible (adjective)

If something is **impossible**, you cannot do it. • *The puzzle was **impossible**.*

> • hopeless • out of the question • unachievable

• Captain Scott's race to the South Pole was a hopeless journey. • Staying up until midnight was out of the question. • The swimmers felt that setting a new world record was unachievable.

> opposites: achievable • possible

incredible (adjective)

Something that is **incredible** is hard to believe. • *The sailor's tales were **incredible**.*

> • unbelievable • implausible • absurd

• My little brother tells unbelievable tales. • Her reasons for missing the appointment were implausible. • No one believed the rascal's absurd story.

> opposites: believable • credible

interesting (adjective)

Something **interesting** holds your attention.
*I'm reading an **interesting** book about insects.*

> • fascinating • compelling • gripping

• Dad thinks bee-keeping is a fascinating hobby.
• The new play has a compelling plot • The film was completely gripping.

> opposites: dull • boring

a
b
c
d
e
f
g
h
i
j
k
l
m
n
o
p
q
r
s
t
u
v
w
x
y
z

Jj

jealous (adjective)

If you are **jealous**, you are angry or upset because someone has something that you want. • *Caroline was **jealous** of Ted's speedy scooter.*

> • envious • resentful

- Beth was envious of her friend's holiday plans.
- He was resentful about Tom's expensive watch.

job (noun)

A **job** is something you do or something you are paid to do.
*Victoria's **job** was as a primary school teacher.*

> • work • chore • task • occupation

- My brother does part-time work at a garage.
- The twins have to do their chores before they go out to play.
- My first task each day is to clean out the rabbit's hutch.
- Chris wants an occupation where she can work with animals.

join (verb)

To **join** means to bring together.
*The boy **joined** the last pieces of the jigsaw.*

> • connect • link • unite

- The bedrooms were connected by a wooden door.
- The train carriages are linked together.
- The ranger tried to unite the lost cub with its mother.

> opposite: separate

joke (noun)

A **joke** is a trick or a story that makes people laugh.
*I tied Dad's shoes together for a **joke**.*

> • jest • prank • gag • wisecrack

- Martin's jest made the teacher laugh.
- Alice played a prank on her mum.
- Dad is always telling gags.
- Jessie's wisecracks hurt my feelings.

jolt (verb)

To **jolt** means to move quickly and suddenly.
*The whole bus **jolted** suddenly when the driver put on the brakes.*

> • bump • jerk • shake

- The old car bumped along the road.
- The train jerked forward as it set off from the station.
- We could feel the house shake during the earthquake.

journey (noun)

When you go on a **journey** you travel somewhere.
*The **journey** to Australia was very long.*

> • trip • voyage • expedition • trek • excursion

- We are going on a trip to Mexico.
- Columbus's first voyage to the New World was in 1492.
- Mary told exciting stories about her expedition to the North Pole.
- The scouts had a long trek ahead of them.
- We went on an excursion to the famous botanical gardens.

judge (verb)

To **judge** something means to make a decision about it.
*A real artist was going to **judge** who had done the best painting.*

> • assess • appraise • evaluate

- The teacher assessed the students' work.
- We tried to appraise the new sculptures in the museum.
- The experts evaluated the antique furniture.

jump (verb)

To **jump** means to leap up into the air.
*Stacey can **jump** quite high on her trampoline.*

> • bounce • hop • leap • spring

- Sam bounced up and down on the bed.
- When Jo hurt her foot she had to hop.
- A leopard can leap up into a tree.
- Ben hid in the wardrobe, ready to spring out on his sister.

Kk

keen (adjective)

If you are **keen**, you are eager. • *Kelly was a **keen** tennis player.*

• avid • eager • enthusiastic • anxious

- My sister is an avid rugby fan. • The librarian was eager to help the trainees.
- Sean was an enthusiastic goalkeeper. • Jane was anxious to impress the judges.

opposite: unenthusiastic

keep (verb)

To **keep** means to have something and not let go of it.
*I **keep** any spare pocket money in my piggy bank.*

• save • reserve • retain

- I saved my sweets to share with my best friend.
- The dancers reserved their best performance for the final show.
- The little girl wanted to retain her library books.

opposites: get rid of • release

kill (verb)

If you **kill** a living thing, it dies. • *The lion **killed** its prey.*

• slay • execute • murder • assassinate

- St George had to slay the dragon. • The prisoner was executed at dawn.
- The police discovered that the victim had been murdered.
- The men plotted to assassinate the president.

kind (adjective)

If you are **kind**, you are gentle and caring.
*A **kind** friend lent me his pencil.*

• compassionate • gentle • loving • considerate

- The compassionate nurse felt sorry for the patient.
- The farmer was gentle with the newborn lamb. • My grandpa is a very loving person.
- It was considerate of Fred to send me some flowers.

opposites: cruel • mean • unkind

kind (noun)

A **kind** is a sort or a type. • *What **kind** of music do you like?*

> • variety • breed • species • type

• Black Dawn is a new variety of tulip. • Rex was a rare breed of dog.
• The explorer discovered a new species of monkey. • Darjeeling is a type of tea.

knot (verb)

If you **knot** a piece of rope or string, you tie it together.
*The sailor **knotted** the rope in seconds.*

> • tie • loop • bind • secure

• "I can tie my shoelaces now!" said Carly.
• Mum looped the string around both packages.
• The nurse had to bind the cut on my hand
with a bandage. • Ben secured his bike to the
fence with a bike chain.

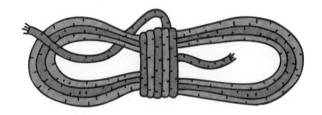

> opposites: unfasten • untie

know (verb)

If you **know** about something, you understand it.
*Do you **know** how to use a computer?*

> • realize • understand • see • be sure of

• The actress didn't realize how late she was.
• The children understood why their mum was so annoyed with them.
• She could see why her maths homework was wrong.
• The angry customer was sure of his facts.

If you **know** someone, you recognize that person.
*Tom **knew** everyone at his party.*

> • identify • recognize • remember

• The woman told the police that she could identify the thief.
• Although the friends had not met for 20 years, they
recognized each other instantly. • Jason remembered
all his team mates from his old club.

Ll

land (noun)

Land is the solid earth under your feet.
*You don't need much **land** to grow vegetables.*

> • ground • soil • earth

• The ground was too hard to dig. • The farmer ploughs the soil with his new tractor.
• The earth began to shake beneath their feet.

land (verb)

To **land** means to stop travelling and come to rest on water or solid ground.
*The helicopter **landed** on the hotel roof.*

> • touch down • arrive • alight

• The plane touched down on the runway.
• The boat arrived at a desert island.
• A wasp alighted on Emma's nose.

> opposite: take off

large (adjective)

If something is **large**, it is very big.
*My aunt received a **large** package in the post.*

> • big • massive • colossal • enormous

• A toucan has a big, colourful beak. • The weightlifter has massive shoulders.
• We looked up at the colossal building. • The giant had enormous feet!

> opposites: little • small • tiny

last (adjective)

If something is **last,** it is the final one.
*The black ant in **last** place was carrying a leaf.*

> • closing • final • concluding

• Ben took the lead in the closing moments of the race. • The penalty kick was the final chance
to win the match. • The concluding episode of the TV series was very exciting.

> opposites: first • initial • opening

last (verb)

If something **lasts**, it stays in place or continues for a length of time.
The house made of stone was built to last.

> • endure • continue • persist

• Shakespeare's work has endured long after his death. • Isabel wanted the music to continue forever. • The tropical rain persisted for three days.

late (adjective)

If you are **late**, you arrive after the agreed time.
Ben was late for his meeting at the bank.

> • behind • delayed • overdue • belated

• I am behind with my school project. • The delayed train arrived two hours late.
• My books are overdue at the library. • I received a belated Christmas present in January.

> opposites: early • on time

laugh (verb)

When you **laugh** you make a happy sound because something is funny.
Amy couldn't stop laughing at her silly cat.

> • chuckle • giggle • guffaw • chortle

• We started to chuckle when we saw the little monster on TV. • I was told off for giggling too loudly in class. • The funny photo made us guffaw. • Everyone chortled at the comedy play.

> opposites: cry • sob • weep

lazy (adjective)

If you are **lazy**, you do not want to do any work.
Jack was a lazy boy who hardly ever left the sofa.

> • idle • slothful • careless • indolent

• Sarah was idle and did not go outside to play. • The slothful boy never tidied his bedroom. • The store's employees had a very careless way of working. • The indolent waitress was always sitting down.

> opposites: active • busy • energetic

Ll

lead (verb)

To **lead** means to show someone the way. • *The guide has to **lead** the tourists past the ruins.*

> • guide • conduct • escort • usher

• She guided the blind man across the street. • The waiter conducted us to our table.
• Charlotte escorted her parents to their seats. • The manager ushered us out of the shop.

> opposite: follow

leave (verb)

When you **leave**, you go away.
*Granny had to **leave**, but she'll visit again next week.*

> • go • depart • set out

• We have to go before it gets dark. • We planned to depart
at six o'clock. • I set out for school straight after breakfast.

> opposites: arrive • come

like (verb)

If you **like** something, you are pleased with it.
*Seals really **like** eating fish.*

> • admire • enjoy • be fond of

• The jeweller admired the new silver brooch. • Grandma enjoys
baking cakes. • Anna is fond of her next-door neighbour.

> opposites: dislike • hate

like (adjective)

If one thing is **like** another, it is the same or similar.
*Mum's new car was **like** her old one.*

> • identical • comparable • similar

• Lisa's outfit was identical to her twin sister's. • The professor's discoveries are comparable
to my own. • My brother looks similar to me.

> opposites: unlike • dissimilar

little (adjective)

If something is **little**, it is small or tiny.
*My puppy was so cute when she was **little**.*

> • small • miniature • minute • tiny

• We planted a small tree in the garden. • I collect miniature teapots.
• The minute beetle crept through the keyhole.
• The baby wore tiny mittens on her hands.

> opposites: big • large

lonely (adjective)

If you are **lonely** you feel sad because you are alone.
*Jim felt **lonely** when all his friends went home.*

> • friendless • alone • solitary • forsaken

• The new girl at school wasn't friendless for long. • The old lady lived alone in a big house.
• The artist was a solitary man. • The puppy felt forsaken when its owner went away.

long (adjective)

If something is **long**, it lasts for more time or distance than usual.
*The monkey had a very **long** tail.*

> • endless • lengthy • extended

• Doing the laundry is an endless task.
• The teacher gave a lengthy explanation about the solar system.
• I took an extended holiday in Australia.

> opposite: short

look (verb)

To **look** means to turn your eyes towards someone or something.
*"**Look** at these footprints!" Jack exclaimed.*

> • examine • gaze • stare • watch

• The doctor had to examine the wound. • The artist gazed at
the beautiful painting. • Dan knew it was rude to stare at people.
• I watched the bird through my binoculars.

a b c d e f g h i j k l m n o p q r s t u v w x y z

lose (verb)

If you **lose** something, you cannot find it. • *My uncle often **loses** his socks in the wardrobe.*

> • misplace • mislay

• Jenny misplaced her locker key for the third time that day.
• Dad mislays his phone all the time.

> opposite: find

loud (adjective)

If something is **loud**, it is very noisy.
*Andrew wears headphones when he listens to **loud** music.*

> • blaring • deafening • noisy • thunderous

• The blaring music disturbed everyone. • A pneumatic drill makes a deafening noise.
• The noisy mob stormed through the streets. • Uncle Jed has a thunderous voice.

> opposites: low • quiet • soft

love (verb)

If you **love** someone or something, that person or thing means a lot to you.
*Daisy **loves** her cat very much.*

> • adore • worship • dote on

• I adore my parents most of the time! • The small boy worships
his older brother. • Professor Williams doted on his students.

> opposite: hate

lovely (adjective)

If something is **lovely**, it is delightful or pretty.
*The bride is wearing a **lovely** silk dress.*

> • attractive • beautiful • exquisite

• Mum wore an attractive hat to the wedding. • Beautiful flowers grow in the garden.
• My sister has some exquisite jewellery.

> opposites: hideous • ugly

magic (noun)

Magic is the power to make something impossible happen.
*The fairy uses **magic** to grant wishes.*

> • sorcery • witchcraft • wizardry

- The puppet was brought to life by sorcery.
- Polly wanted to learn about witchcraft.
- "My wizardry will turn you into a frog!" cackled the wizard.

main (adjective)

Main means the most important.
*I played the **main** character in the school play.*

> • chief • principal • prime • head

- "The chief problem is the leaking roof," said the builder.
- The principal ballerina is very tall. • Roger the Robber is our prime suspect.
- I addressed my letter to the head of the company.

> opposite: minor

make (verb)

To **make** means to force a person or an object to do something.
*"Please don't **make** me go to the spooky house!" squealed Rosie.*

> • compel • force • oblige

- The rain compelled me to put up my umbrella.
- Sam's brother forced him to tell lies.
- "Don't oblige me to separate you," warned the teacher.

When you **make** something, you build it or put it together.
*Lewis likes to **make** towers out of bricks.*

> • create • build • produce

- Max created a robot out of junk.
- "I want to build a sandcastle," said Tim.
- The big factory produces cars.

> opposite: destroy

Mm

many (adjective)

Many means a large number of something.
*"There are too **many** cars on the road today,"* Paul complained.

> • abundant • countless • numerous • lots

- The farmer grew an abundant crop of sweetcorn.
- Joe made countless trips to the sweet shop.
- The class read numerous books about space.
- There were lots of skateboards for sale.

> opposite: few

mark (noun)

A **mark** is a dirty spot.
*I scrubbed the oily **marks** off my jeans.*

> • stain • smudge • spot • smear

- The stain would not come out of her evening gown.
- The artist made a smudge on his drawing.
- I have a spot on my silk tie.
- We found a large smear on the window.

match (noun)

A **match** is an event in which two people,
or two teams, play against each other.
*The whole family went to the **match**.*

> • competition • contest • game

- We cheered when our team won the competition.
- She challenged me to a skipping contest. • The board game lasted for hours.

matter (noun)

A **matter** is a subject that you need to think about or act upon.
*"We should talk about this **matter**,"* said the doctor.

> • issue • topic • subject

- The most important issue was the increase in nuclear power. • Our school held a debate on the topic of recycling. • Martin is passionate about the subject of politics.

a b c d e f g h i j k l **m** n o p q r s t u v w x y z

meal (noun)

A **meal** is the food that you sit down to eat at different times of the day.
*"Breakfast is my favourite **meal** of the day," said Mum.*

> • feast • snack • banquet

- A delicious feast was spread out on the blanket.
- We had a quick snack on our way to the airport.
- The king held a banquet for his guests.

mean (adjective)

If you are **mean**, you are unkind to others.
*A girl at school was really **mean** to me today.*

> • nasty • unfriendly • cruel • selfish

- Mum told me not to be nasty to my little sister.
- Stay away from that dog - it looks unfriendly.
- We should never be cruel to animals.
- Thomas was selfish and wouldn't share his toys.

> opposites: kind • friendly • generous

mean (verb)

To **mean** something is to try to express a particular thing.
*"I don't understand what you **mean**," said the student.*

> • imply • indicate • signify

- His smile implied that he was joking.
- A red light indicates that you must stop.
- Dark clouds signify that it is going to rain.

meet (verb)

To **meet** is to come together.
*"Let's **meet** at the cinema," suggested Annie.*

> • assemble • gather • congregate

- The crowd assembled outside the town hall.
- We gather in the playground every morning.
- Maisy's friends congregated in front of her house.

Mm

melt (verb)

To **melt** is to change to a liquid when heated.
*My ice cream **melted** quickly in the sunshine.*

> • dissolve • defrost • thaw

• Sugar dissolves in a hot cup of tea. • I defrost my dinner in the microwave.
• Ice thaws when the sun comes out.

> opposites: freeze • harden

mend (verb)

To **mend** something means to repair it. • *Matt tried to **mend** his mum's broken vase.*

> • repair • fix

• The builders repaired the hole in the roof. • "I've fixed the motorcycle!" grinned the mechanic.

> opposite: break

mess (noun)

A **mess** is an untidy confusion of things.
*"Clean up this **mess**!" yelled Mum.*

> • chaos • shambles • jumble • clutter

• The room was in chaos after the party.
• "My desk is a shambles," cried May.
• We helped sort out the jumble of clothes.
• The kitchen table was buried under the clutter.

> opposites: order • tidiness

middle (noun)

The **middle** is the point that is halfway between two other points.
*I never eat the pips in the **middle** of my apple.*

> • centre • core • heart

• My favourite chocolates have strawberry centres.
• It is very hot at the Earth's core.
• The statue stands in the heart of our city.

mild (adjective)

If something is **mild**, it is gentle.
*There was a **mild** breeze as we sailed out to sea.*

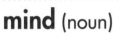

● gentle ● serene ● pleasant

- Annabelle is a very gentle person.
- Our horse has a serene temperament.
- "We had pleasant weather on our holiday," smiled George.

mind (noun)

Your **mind** is the part of you that lets you think, feel, remember and understand.
*Jake's clever **mind** soon figured out the puzzle.*

● brain ● intellect ● intelligence

- My brain was tired after a day of studying!
- "Use your intellect to answer the question," said Mr Mason.
- Everyone admired the smart child's sharp intelligence.

miss (verb)

To **miss** is to feel sad because a person or thing is no longer present.
*Carl **missed** the mountains when he went to live in the city.*

● pine ● long for ● want

- The dog pined for its owners when they went away.
- When I moved school I longed for my old friends.
- Mark was homesick and wanted his mum.

If you **miss**, you fail to find or hit a target.
*We all groaned when Harry **missed** an easy shot.*

● avoid ● evade ● dodge

- We left early to avoid the rush hour.
- The crafty jewel thief evaded the police.
- "No one is going to dodge sports day!"
shouted the PE teacher.

opposites: find ● hit

Mm

mistake (noun)

A **mistake** is something that you do wrong.
*I made a basic **mistake** in my maths test.*

> • blunder • error • oversight

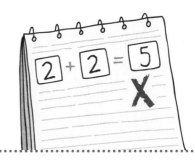

- The clumsy man apologized for his blunder.
- "I made an error when I trusted you," snapped the supervisor.
- Ben didn't receive his invitation due to an oversight.

mix (verb)

To **mix** means to put together.
*Alfie **mixed** the blue and red paints to make purple.*

> • blend • combine • mingle • merge

- We blend letter sounds to make words in our phonics class.
- You combine butter, sugar, eggs and flour to make a cake.
- The funny clown mingled with the audience.
- All the classes merged for a dancing lesson.

> opposite: separate

moan (noun)

A **moan** is an unhappy sound that shows you are in pain or in trouble.
*The patient gave a **moan** as the doctor touched his stomach.*

> • groan • wail • sob • whine

- We heard a groan coming from the cupboard. • I let out a wail when I saw the ghost!
- My sister's loud sob woke me up. • The dog's whine was a horrible noise.

modern (adjective)

If something is **modern** it is up to date.
***Modern** trains can travel up to 200 km per hour.*

> • latest • contemporary • fashionable • current

- "I only wear the latest clothes," said the model. • The contemporary furniture looked odd in the old house. • My aunt wears fashionable shoes. • I like to read books by current writers.

> opposites: dated • old-fashioned

money (noun)

Money is what is used to buy things.
*I earn extra **money** by delivering newspapers.*

> • cash • change • funds • riches

- Dad gave me some cash to buy new trainers.
- "Have you got any change for the vending machine?" Kathy asked.
- He saved up his funds to buy a new car.
- All the king's riches couldn't buy him what he wanted.

monster (noun)

A **monster** is an imaginary beast.
*I read about **monsters** in my book of fairy tales.*

> • giant • beast • ogre • troll

- Jack climbed the beanstalk to the giant's castle.
- The wild beast roamed free in the woods
- The book was about a terrifying ogre.
- "A troll lives under that bridge," said Harry.

move (verb)

To **move** is to change the place or position of something.
*"**Move** your feet in time to the beat!" cried the dance instructor.*

> • carry • push • transfer • shift

- Removal men often carry sofas down stairs.
- "Push those boxes out of the way!" said Dad.
- I transferred the heavy bag to my other hand.
- John shifted things around his office.

mystery (noun)

A **mystery** is something puzzling that you cannot explain.
*The writer was working on a **mystery** story.*

> • puzzle • riddle • enigma

- A smart girl solved the puzzle of Grace's missing glasses.
- "I love a good riddle," chuckled my uncle.
- Our new science teacher was something of an enigma.

Nn

narrow (adjective)

If something is **narrow**, it is small in width.
*The pink building was **narrower** than the others on the street.*

> • thin • slender • slim

• Canal boats are long and thin. • Giraffes have long,
slender necks. • My dad is the slim man with the dark hair.

> opposites: broad • wide

nasty (adjective)

To be **nasty** means to be very unpleasant. • *The **nasty** girl hit her little brother.*

> • spiteful • unkind • vile • vicious

• Ethan is a spiteful boy. • "Don't be so unkind," said Archie.
• My vile cousin always pulls my hair. • Martha had a vicious temper.

> opposites: nice • kind • pleasant

naughty (adjective)

To be **naughty** means to behave badly.
*A **naughty** puppy destroyed my favourite teddy bear.*

> • disobedient • bad • impish

• Ted was disobedient and broke the rules. • The bad children tired
out their babysitter. • The impish child was always in trouble.

> opposites: good • polite • well-behaved

near (preposition)

Near means close to something.
*"I love living **near** the sea," said the old sailor.*

> • adjacent • beside • close • neighbouring

• The two houses had adjacent front doors. • Molly sat down beside a stream.
• Jenny lived close to her best friend. • Henry threw rubbish into the neighbouring garden.

> opposites: distant • far

neat (adjective)

To be **neat** means to be tidy.
*The decorator's work was always **neat**.*

> • tidy • orderly • well-kept

• David liked to keep his room tidy. • "It is important to be orderly,"
said the captain. • The gardens looked colourful and well-kept.

> opposite: messy • untidy

need (verb)

To **need** means to require something.
*"I **need** more flour for this recipe," sighed Jim.*

> • crave • require

• "I crave peace and quiet," said Helen.
• To make a greetings card you require paper, a pencil and some paints.

nervous (adjective)

To be **nervous** is to be easily scared or worried.
*Sarah felt too **nervous** to get into the pool.*

> • anxious • uneasy • timid • edgy

• Alice was anxious about her science test. • Grandma was
uneasy about flying in a plane. • Mice are timid creatures.
• I felt edgy when I heard the door creak open.

> opposites: calm • relaxed

new (adjective)

If something is **new** it has just been made, thought of or bought.
*Aunt Jessie bought me some cool **new** trainers!*

> • fresh • original • novel

• The teacher asked for some fresh ideas. • We saw an original
play at the theatre. • Norman has a novel diet plan.

> opposite: old

Nn

next (adjective)

The **next** is the one that comes right after. • *We waited to catch the **next** bus.*

> • subsequent • following • later

• Subsequent to the accident, everyone was more careful. • The circus arrived the following day.
• "I'll take the later train," said Jack.

> opposite: previous

nice (adjective)

Something that is **nice** is pleasing.
*Abbie had a **nice** time ice skating.*

> • pleasant • agreeable • charming

• The house had a pleasant garden. • The weather was very agreeable that day. • The charming boy shook hands with the visitor.

> opposites: nasty • horrid • unpleasant

noisy (adjective)

If something is **noisy**, it is too loud.
*"You're being too **noisy**!" Maya's dad told her.*

> • deafening • loud • strident • piercing

• The music at the disco was deafening. • The jet's engines made a loud noise as the plane landed.
• "You've got a very strident voice," said the nurse. • Shelley let out a piercing scream.

> opposite: quiet

nonsense (noun)

Words, actions or ideas that are **nonsense** are silly or have no meaning.
*Mr Lewin said that Robert's story was a lot of **nonsense**.*

> • gibberish • drivel • silliness

• The boys were talking gibberish to each other. • "What drivel!" snapped the teacher.
• There was much silliness at Samir's party.

> opposite: sense

normal (adjective)

If something is **normal**, it is usual and what you would expect.
*The school bus left at the **normal** time.*

> • usual • ordinary • regular • average

• The usual driver was on holiday. • The magician held up an ordinary wooden box.
• I bought a regular-size milkshake. • "He's an average student," said the music teacher.

> opposites: strange • abnormal

nosy (adjective)

To be **nosy** is to snoop or interfere.
*We live next door to a very **nosy** neighbour!*

> • prying • snooping

• I hid my designs away from prying eyes.
• The snooping detective found all the clues he needed.

> opposite: uninterested

notice (verb)

To **notice** is to see or observe.
*Eileen **noticed** a rare butterfly in the garden.*

> • spot • observe • detect

• "Did you spot me on TV?" asked William.
• Road users must observe the Highway Code.
• We all detected a strange smell.

> opposite: miss

nuisance (noun)

A **nuisance** is something or someone that is annoying.
*The roadworks were a terrible **nuisance**.*

> • pest • irritation

• "Don't be such a pest!" yelled my brother.
• The sound of car alarms going off is a big irritation.

Oo

object (noun)

The **object** is the main purpose or target.
*The **object** of a game of baseball is to score a home run.*

> • aim • goal • purpose

- Jim's aim in life was to be a success.
- Mum's goal was to decorate the whole house.
- The purpose of going to the market was to buy some fruit.

An **object** is a thing you can touch and see.
*I had to guess what the **object** was with my eyes closed.*

> • article • thing • item

- Megan was wearing ten different articles of clothing. • "What's that thing on the table?"
Jo asked. • There were five items in the shopping basket.

odd (adjective)

If something is **odd**, it is different or unusual.
*The carrots we grew were a very **odd** shape.*

> • weird • bizarre • peculiar • strange

- Andrea dyed her hair a weird colour.
- "What a bizarre boat!" exclaimed the sailor.
- Callum's peculiar accent was hard to understand.
- A strange noise came from the cupboard.

> opposite: normal

often (adverb)

Often means frequently.
*Jen **often** fed the penguins and seals at the zoo.*

> • frequently • much • repeatedly

- The buses to town run frequently.
- Shakespeare is a much-quoted writer.
- Dave recited the poem repeatedly.

> opposites: rarely • seldom

old (adjective)

Something **old** has existed for a long time. • *Tony wore an old jumper for painting.*

> • aged • ancient • elderly

• The aged wizard had a long white beard. • There is an ancient ruin on the hill.
• My grandma is an elderly lady.

> opposites: new • young

If something is **old**, it is the one that came before. • *Our old house had four bedrooms.*

> • earlier • former • previous

• "This phone is better than the earlier model," said Ron. • Andy's former job was driving a bus.
• My previous teacher was very kind.

> opposites: current • present

once (adverb)

Once means at one time in the past.
I once saw an alien spaceship.

> • formerly • previously

• Mrs Evans was formerly a nurse. • Our house was previously a monastery.

only (adjective)

If something is **only** it is a single one. • *Dan was an only child.*

> • lone • single • sole

• She was the lone girl in the swimming team. • I had a single coin left in my purse.
• The waiter was the sole witness to the crime.

only (adverb)

Only means nothing more than. • *There were only two crisps left in the bag.*

> • just • merely

• We had just 30 seconds to answer the question.
• "You're merely a child," said the nasty man.

Oo

open (verb)

To **open** means to move or change from a closed position.
*Bert **opened** the door to the postman.*

> • unwrap • unfasten • unfold

- Mary unwrapped her presents excitedly.
- The burglar unfastened the window.
- Uncle Mike unfolded the map.

> opposites: close • shut

open (adjective)

If something is **open** it is not closed or locked.
*"The shop is **open** for business," said the sales assistant.*

> • ajar • unlocked • gaping

- My bedroom door was ajar. • The toy cupboard was unlocked.
- The dentist looked into my gaping mouth.

order (verb)

To **order** means to command.
*Sergeant Brown **ordered** his soldiers to salute.*

> • command • direct • charge • instruct

- The queen commanded everyone to kneel.
- The captain directed his crew to abandon ship.
- "I charge you to tell the truth!" yelled the judge.
- Mum instructed the delivery men to put the bed upstairs.

ordinary (adjective)

If something is **ordinary** it is normal or expected.
*Mary wore an **ordinary** coat.*

> • everyday • normal • usual • standard

- A cold is an everyday illness. • The patient's temperature was normal.
- I finished school at the usual time today. • White is the standard colour for a dishwasher.

> opposites: extraordinary • unusual

74

organize (verb)

To **organize** means to plan something and work out the details.
*I **organized** the school disco.*

> • arrange • coordinate • run

- Uncle Bruno arranged a surprise party.
- The police coordinated a search of a wide area.
- Miss Block runs the village fete every year.

out (adverb)

If you are **out**, you are not at home or in a particular place.
*I went to see my best friend but she was **out**.*

> • absent • away • elsewhere

- Natalie was absent from school on Monday.
- We went away on holiday for two weeks.
- The angry customer said she would shop elsewhere.

> opposites: here • in • present

outing (noun)

If you go on an **outing**, you take a short, fun trip.
*We brought our tent on an **outing** to the countryside.*

> • trip • excursion • tour

- Our school took us on a trip to the zoo.
- We organized an excursion to the museum.
- Mum went on a tour of Paris.

over (adjective)

If something is **over**, it is in the past.
*We got up when the film was **over**.*

> • finished • completed • ended

- We will celebrate when our final exam has finished.
- I completed the task yesterday.
- Our fun ended when the teacher came in.

Pp

painful (adjective)

If something is **painful**, it hurts.
*My arm was **painful**, so the nurse gave me some medicine.*

> • aching • sore • stinging • throbbing

- The young athlete's legs were aching.
- The skier's bruises were very sore.
- The child rubbed her stinging eyes.
- "I've got a throbbing headache," Bella complained.

> opposite: painless

part (noun)

A **part** is a section of a whole thing.
*They could only eat **part** of the cake.*

> • piece • portion • segment • fragment

- "Have another piece of pizza," said Uncle Roy.
- Marcus saved a portion of pie for his brother.
- We shared the segments of the orange.
- Only a fragment of the original letter from Captain Cook was left.

pass (verb)

To **pass** means to move by something.
*I saw a train **pass** while I was collecting my ticket.*

> • go by • outdo • outstrip

- I was scared to go by the old haunted house.
- I'd like to outdo my best score at netball.
- Zoe outstripped all her friends in the hurdles race.

To **pass** means to transfer or exchange an item.
*Jack **passed** the book to his teacher.*

> • give • hand • transfer

- "Give me that pencil," said Jennifer rudely.
- We handed the fossil around the class.
- I transferred schools halfway through the term.

peaceful (adjective)

Peaceful means quiet and calm.
*Libraries are **peaceful** places.*

> • quiet • restful • serene

- Grandma's garden is lovely and quiet.
- Mum felt better after a restful sleep.
- The old woman had a serene face.

> opposites: disturbed • noisy

perfect (adjective)

If something is **perfect**, it has no faults. • *Beth's saxophone solo was **perfect**.*

> • faultless • exact • flawless • excellent

- The pianist gave a faultless performance at the concert. • Jill drew an exact copy of the picture.
- The flawless diamond was worth a fortune. • My new watch keeps excellent time.

> opposites: imperfect • wrong

pick (verb)

To **pick** means to choose or select. • *Ellie was asked to **pick** players for her team.*

> • choose • decide on • select • opt for

- Dad always lets Mum choose the restaurant. • Daryl decided on the white trainers.
- I want to select a new carpet for my bedroom. • Greg always opts for chocolate ice cream.

> opposite: reject

piece (noun)

A **piece** is a part or a bit of something.
*The waitress gave me a **piece** of apple pie.*

> • bit • chunk • scrap • segment

- The mouse took a bit of cheese.
- Daniel handed me a chunk of chocolate.
- She picked up a scrap of paper from the floor.
- I ate several segments of grapefruit for breakfast.

Pp

pile (noun)

A **pile** is a heap of something.
*There's a **pile** of dirty pots in the sink.*

> • mound • mountain • stack

- The dog dug out a huge mound of soil in the garden.
- "I have a mountain of homework to do," groaned Violet.
- The doctor received a stack of mail in the post each morning.

place (noun)

A **place** is a particular area.
*My home town is an interesting **place**.*

> • spot • location • position

• We found a good spot to set up our tent. • Tony's company moved to a new location in the city centre. • The hiker marked his exact position on the map.

place (verb)

To **place** means to put.
*We always **place** our books on the bookshelf after reading.*

> • put • rest • lay

- "Please put on your coat," said Mum.
- I rested my hands on Clare's shoulders.
- "Can you lay the baby in her cot?" asked Dad.

play (verb)

To **play** means to amuse yourself or to join in a game.
*Annie would happily **play** on her own.*

> • have fun • frolic • romp about

- The twins love having fun with their friends.
- Lambs frolic in the fields in spring.
- The boys like to romp about in the garden.

> opposite: work

please (verb)

To **please** someone means to make them happy.
*Ryan's kindness **pleased** his mother.*

> • satisfy • gladden • thrill

- Eve can never satisfy her teacher. • It gladdens me to hear birds singing.
- The ballet dancer thrilled the audience with her performance.

> opposite: displease

poor (adjective)

If you are **poor** you have little or no money or things.
*The old man was **poor** but happy.*

> • penniless • destitute • needy

- She was penniless after giving away all her money.
- The destitute family had nowhere to live.
- It is kind to give money to needy people.

> opposites: rich • wealthy

pretty (adjective)

If something is **pretty** it is pleasant to look at.
*The **pretty** young mermaid sat on the rocks.*

> • beautiful • lovely • gorgeous • attractive

- Jill had beautiful dark-brown hair. • Grandma bought some lovely silk curtains.
- Mr and Mrs Blake lived in a gorgeous cottage. • Jack was an attractive boy.

> opposite: ugly

problem (noun)

A **problem** is a difficulty or question.
*Sam had a **problem** with the saddle on his bike.*

> • trouble • complication • worry

- "What's the trouble?" asked Mum. • The operation went without complication.
- My main worry was that I wouldn't pass my maths test.

a b c d e f g h i j k l m n o p q r s t u v w x y z

protect (verb)

To **protect** means to keep something safe from harm.
*The enclosure on our trampoline is there to **protect** us.*

> • defend • guard • shelter • shield

• The soldiers fired arrows to defend the castle. • Special officers guard the king and queen.
• The cat sheltered her kittens from the rain. • I shielded my friend from the bullies.

> opposites: attack • threaten

proud (adjective)

To be **proud** means to be pleased with yourself or someone else for doing well.
*Jim was **proud** of himself for finishing the fun run.*

> • boastful • pleased • satisfied

• Mr Green was boastful about his clever daughter. • The students were pleased with their test results. • The girl was satisfied with her performance at the concert.

> opposite: humble

pull (verb)

To **pull** means to drag something or someone towards you.
*The door was stuck, and I had to **pull** hard to open it.*

> • drag • tow • haul • tug

• Beth had to drag her heavy bag upstairs. • Our car tows the trailer along the road.
• The teacher hauled me out of the pool. • I had to tug at the lead to get my dog to move.

> opposite: push

push (verb)

To **push** means to force someone or something away from you.
*Gemma **pushed** the train along the track.*

> • thrust • shove

• I thrust a coin into my brother's hand. • Mum shoved her way to the front of the line.

> opposite: pull

Qq

question (verb)

To **question** means to ask or enquire.
*The teacher **questioned** us about our holidays.*

> • ask • interrogate • quiz

- "I want to ask you about this broken window," said our neighbour.
- The police officer interrogated his suspect. • We were quizzed about the missing cakes.

quick (adjective)

If you are **quick**, you are speedy.
*Carl finished first in the race because he was so **quick**.*

> • swift • fast • brisk • rapid

- Toby made a swift exit when the meeting finished.
- Cheetahs are really fast runners. • Dad goes for a brisk walk every morning. • "I am a rapid reader," boasted Michelle.

> opposite: slow

quiet (adjective)

To be **quiet** means to make little or no sound.
*A mouse is a **quiet** animal.*

> • hushed • noiseless • silent • soundless

- People speak in hushed voices in church.
- Charlotte tiptoed on noiseless feet.
- "Be silent!" ordered Mr Williams. • The deer was soundless as it ran across the field.

> opposites: loud • noisy

quite (adjective)

Quite can mean completely and utterly. • *The magician was **quite** amazing.*

> • absolutely • completely • totally • fully

- I was absolutely sure I had the correct answer.
- "I completely agree," said the shop manager.
- Our crossword answers were totally wrong.
- The firefighters were fully aware of the risks.

a b c d e f g h i j k l m n o p q r s t u v w x y z

Rr

rain (noun)

Rain is water that falls from the clouds.
*Nyla loved splashing in the **rain** and mud!*

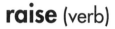
- shower • downpour • drizzle

- The shower did not last long.
- "You're not going out in this downpour," said Mum.
- I was on my way home when the drizzle began.

raise (verb)

To **raise** means to lift upwards. • *The nurse had to **raise** Simon's broken leg.*

- elevate • escalate • lift

- If you elevate your sprained ankle it will feel better. • Our local supermarket has escalated its prices. • Beth asked her dad to lift her on to his shoulders.

opposite: lower

ready (adjective)

If something is **ready**, it is prepared to do something or to be used.
*"Your dinner is almost **ready**!" called Mum.*

- set • primed • prepared

- We were set to leave when Dad lost the map.
- The class was primed for action.
- "Are you prepared to face the enemy?" asked the captain.

opposites: unprepared • unready

real (adjective)

If something is **real**, it is genuine and not made up.
*Paula's wedding ring had a **real** diamond in it.*

- genuine • true • honest • sincere

- The handbag was made of genuine leather. • My dad is a fireman and a true hero.
- "It was an honest mistake!" cried Elaine. • Michael offered his friends a sincere apology.

opposite: fake

refuse (verb)

To **refuse** means to say "no".
*The toddler **refused** to eat his dinner.*

> • decline • deny • spurn

- Mary declined another cup of tea. • A guard denied us entry to the palace.
- The proud girl spurned my help.

> opposite: accept

relax (verb)

To **relax** means to play or take a rest from work.
*I love to **relax** with a good adventure story.*

> • unwind • laze • rest • calm down

- I unwind by playing chess.
- The dog likes to laze on my bed.
- Sean tried to rest after working in the garden.
- "I wish you would all calm down!" said the teacher.

remember (verb)

If you **remember** something, you keep it in your memory.
*George **remembered** to clean his teeth twice a day.*

> • recall • recollect

- Grandpa can recall the names of his school teachers.
- "I don't recollect inviting you," said Peter rudely.

> opposite: forget

rescue (verb)

To **rescue** means to save a person, animal or thing from danger or harm.
*The firefighter managed to **rescue** the cat from up a tree.*

> • free • salvage • save

- The man tried to free his friend from the trap.
- We could not salvage our furniture from the flood.
- The coastguard saves the lives of many people every year.

83

Rr

respect (verb)

To **respect** someone means to look up to them.
*"You should **respect** your elders," said the old man.*

> • admire • value • revere

- Lloyd admires his father's courage.
- I value my friends' opinions.
- The young sailors revered their captain.

> opposite: disrespect

rest (noun)

A **rest** is a period of relaxing or sleeping.
*Brody went for a **rest** in bed.*

> • nap • sleep • break

- Grandma takes a nap every afternoon.
- The short sleep did the toddler good.
- "Take a break," said the dancing teacher.

The **rest** is what is left over.
*The porter carried three bags while I took the **rest**.*

> • remainder • surplus • balance

- I ate the remainder of the chocolate cake.
- There was a surplus of fruit in the orchard this harvest.
- The last ship carried the balance of the cargo.

rich (adjective)

If you are **rich**, you have lots of money or possessions.
*The man was so **rich**, he bought a castle.*

> • wealthy • affluent • well-to-do

- The wealthy couple own a private jet.
- My aunt is an affluent woman.
- The well-to-do girls wear expensive clothes.

> opposite: poor

right (adjective)

If something is **right**, it is correct. • *I hoped I had the **right** answer.*

> • accurate • correct • exact • precise

• The fortune-teller was accurate. • Jane gave the correct answer to the question.
• I gave the customer the exact change. • "What is the precise time?" asked Ellie.

> opposite: wrong

risk (noun)

A **risk** is a chance of loss or danger.
*We never take **risks** when crossing the road.*

> • gamble • chance • danger • hazard

• I took a gamble and decided to trust him. • There was a chance
that the tyres might slip on the ice. • The factory fire was a danger
to the houses nearby. • The oil spill presented a hazard to wildlife.

> opposite: certainty

rough (adjective)

If something is **rough**, it is uneven or harsh to the touch.
*The garden path had a **rough** surface.*

> • bumpy • craggy • stony

• He drove the tractor across the bumpy field. • A puffin perched on the craggy cliff.
• The plants could not grow in the stony ground.

> opposite: smooth

round (adjective)

Something that is **round** is shaped like a circle.
*In archery, you must try to hit a **round** target.*

> • circular • curved • spiral

• The play was performed on a circular stage.
• The bird had a small curved beak.
• There was a spiral staircase in the old mansion.

Rr

row (noun)

A **row** is a line of people or objects.
The sunflowers in the garden grew in a row.

> • chain • line • column

- I passed the bucket along the chain of people.
- Margaret has a line of seashells on her window sill.
- A column of tanks rumbled slowly north.

rubbish (noun)

Rubbish is something you don't need and throw away.
We put our rubbish in the bin.

> • litter • refuse • waste • debris

- You should never drop litter on the pavement. • Our refuse is collected by a lorry.
- We try to recycle our waste. • The builders cleared away the debris.

rude (adjective)

If you are **rude**, you are impolite.
The rude boy stuck out his tongue at me.

> • bad-mannered • curt • surly • insulting

- The bad-mannered girl shouted at her mum.
- "Shut up, will you!" said Robin in a curt voice.
- I did not like the reporter's surly tone.
- The sergeant spoke in an insulting way.

> opposite: polite

ruin (verb)

To **ruin** something means to damage it so it can't be fixed.
The mud on Mike's boots ruined the new carpet.

> • wreck • demolish • spoil • destroy

- Cara wanted to wreck my stamp collection.
- A huge wave demolished our sandcastle.
- The ugly building spoiled the beautiful view.
- The invading army destroyed the palace.

rule (noun)

A **rule** is an instruction that tells you what you may or may not do.
*We learned the **rules** before we played the game.*

> • law • regulation • decree

- The police make sure that people obey the law.
- There are strict regulations against cruelty to animals.
- In the fairy tale, the king decrees that there are to be no spinning wheels in his kingdom.

rule (verb)

To **rule** something means to be in charge of it.
*"I **rule** this country!" the king declared proudly.*

> • control • govern • lead

- The pilot controls the aeroplane.
- The people wanted to govern their own country themselves.
- A young woman called Sarah leads the reading group.

run (verb)

To **run** means to move quickly.
*Eleanor had two laps left to **run** in her race.*

> • sprint • dart • dash • scamper

- I can sprint faster than all my friends.
- Ben had to dart undercover when it started to rain.
- He dashed to the store before it closed.
- The kittens scampered around the room.

rush (verb)

To **rush** means to hurry.
*We had to **rush** to get to the airport on time.*

> • hurry • fly • scramble

- Everyone hurried home after school.
- "I must fly!" said Mrs Harris when it started to rain.
- We scrambled to be first in line for tickets.

> opposites: dawdle • linger

a b c d e f g h i j k l m n o p q r s t u v w x y z

Ss

sad (adjective)

To be **sad** means to be unhappy. • *Ali was **sad** when his favourite toy broke.*

> • unhappy • miserable • blue

• Dad was unhappy because his car had broken down. • The girl was miserable because her holiday was over. • Connor felt blue when his dog went missing.

> opposites: cheerful • glad • happy

safe (adjective)

If something is **safe,** it is free from danger or harm.
*We lock our bikes in the shed to keep them **safe**.*

> • secure • protected • unharmed

• I felt secure when all the doors were locked. • The princess was always protected from danger.
• "Make sure the animals are unharmed," said the zookeeper.

> opposites: dangerous • unsafe

same (adjective)

Things that are the **same** are exactly like each other.
*The two pilots wear the **same** uniform.*

> • alike • identical • matching

• My mum and her older sister look alike. • My brother and I are identical twins. • I never wear matching socks!

> opposite: different

save (verb)

To **save** means to store something for use in the future.
*Megan wanted to **save** her money.*

> • keep • hoard • hold on to

• I keep all my old cinema tickets. • Misers like to hoard their money.
• Tim held on to his allowance so he could buy his mum a present.

> opposites: spend • waste

say (verb)

To **say** means to speak words. • *Ruby would not **say** where she had been.*

> • utter • state • remark • exclaim

• The stranger did not utter a word. • "Please state your name," said the judge.
• The babysitter remarked that it was bedtime. • "Leave me alone!" I exclaimed.

scare (verb)

To **scare** means to frighten. • *Billy put on a vampire mask to **scare** me.*

> • alarm • terrify • startle

• "Don't alarm Grandma by shouting," warned Dad. • Fireworks terrify my pet cat.
• I was startled by the loud bang.

scream (verb)

To **scream** means to yell loudly.
*Alan **screamed** when he saw the mouse.*

> • yell • screech • shriek

• I yelled as the car rolled backwards. • "Don't screech in
my ear!" complained Mum. • The sick baby shrieked for hours.

secret (adjective)

If something is **secret**, it is not to be told or shown to others.
*James whispered the **secret** password in his friend's ear.*

> • private • concealed • hidden • unknown

• I write my private thoughts in my diary. • "I'll put your jewels in the concealed safe," said the
manager. • The desk has a hidden compartment. • Maisy's unknown admirer sent her red roses.

see (verb)

To **see** means to observe with your eyes.
*I can **see** for miles through my telescope.*

> • glimpse • spot • witness

• Rowan did not glimpse any fairies. • "Did you spot the butterfly?"
asked Mum eagerly. • I witnessed the man stealing a bike.

a b c d e f g h i j k l m n o p q r s t u v w x y z

selfish (adjective)

To be **selfish** means to think only about your own needs and wishes.
*It was **selfish** of Owen to drink all the juice.*

> • greedy • self-centred • ungenerous

• The greedy woman left no food for the children. • David was self-centred, but he wasn't cruel.
• An ungenerous person had taken the last blanket.

> opposite: generous

send (verb)

To **send** something means to direct it to another place.
*Daisy wanted to **send** her best friend a postcard.*

> • post • dispatch • forward • transmit

• I post a card to my aunt on her birthday. • People dispatch thousands of packages every day.
• I forwarded my boss his mail. • The football match was transmitted live by satellite.

> opposite: receive

sensible (adjective)

If something is **sensible**, it is wise. • *It is **sensible** to wear warm clothes in the winter.*

> • wise • practical • reasonable

• The professor always gives wise advice. • The builder had some practical ideas.
• It was reasonable to ask for a lunch break.

> opposites: silly • unwise

serious (adjective)

If something is **serious**, it is important or worrying.
*Nancy almost had a **serious** crash on her bike.*

> • grave • solemn • long-faced

• Dad looked grave when he told us the bad news. • We were very solemn
when we met the judge. • The long-faced man did not laugh at the joke.

> opposite: light-hearted

shake (verb)

To **shake** means to move quickly up and down or back and forth.
*I told Gary to **shake** the ketchup bottle.*

> • quiver • shiver • shudder • tremble

- I saw the leaves quiver in the breeze.
- Most people shiver if they are cold.
- Scary stories can make you shudder.
- The little dog trembled with fear.

share (verb)

To **share** means to divide something between a number of people.
*We **shared** the last slice of chocolate cake.*

> • divide • split • distribute

- Dad divided the prize money between us.
- The teacher split the class into smaller groups.
- The jobs were distributed among the three men.

sharp (adjective)

If something is **sharp**, it is pointed and could cut you.
*The kitchen knife was extremely **sharp**.*

> • pointed • cutting

- The seamstress pricked her finger on the pointed needle.
- "The cutting edges of scissors are dangerous," said the teacher.

> opposite: blunt

shine (verb)

If something **shines**, it glows brightly.
*Chloe **shines** her torch to help her read at night.*

> • beam • gleam • glitter • sparkle

- The moonlight beams through my curtains.
- A light was gleaming in the library window.
- The little girl's eyes glittered with excitement.
- Sunlight sparkled on the water.

Ss

short (adjective)

Something **short** is less than the usual height or length.
*Jessie's little brother is **short** for his age.*

> • little • small • squat

• I bought a little tree to plant in my garden. • "You are too small to go on that ride," the man told Jamie. • Our neighbour is a squat woman.

> opposites: long • tall

shout (verb)

To **shout** means to call out loudly.
*Ben had to **shout** to make his grandad hear.*

> • bellow • yell • bawl • roar

• The coach had to bellow at the players. • Dad began to yell when his team scored.
• I bawled at my friend across the playground. • "Don't do that!" roared the teacher.

> opposite: whisper

show (verb)

To **show** means to allow something to be seen.
*Anna was proud to **show** the whole class her certificate.*

> • reveal • display • present

• I pulled off my mask to reveal my face. • Maggie displays her sculptures in the art gallery. • The lawyer presented her evidence to the jury.

> opposite: hide

shy (adjective)

A **shy** person is nervous with strangers. • *My **shy** cousin blushed when I spoke to her.*

> • timid • bashful • meek

• The timid dog put his tail between his legs. • Lewis was bashful around girls.
• "Yes, sir," said the boy, in a meek voice.

> opposites: outgoing • bold • confident

silent (adjective)

To be **silent** means to make no noise. • *Nina was **silent** for almost an hour.*

> • quiet • noiseless • soundless

• "Be quiet!" snapped the headteacher. • The burglars were noiseless when they broke into the house. • Noah danced on soundless feet.

> opposite: noisy

silly (adjective)

If something is **silly**, it is not sensible.
*The circus clown put on a **silly** show.*

> • absurd • foolish • idiotic • unwise

• "That's an absurd idea!" laughed Sonia. • Oliver made a foolish decision.
• Our idiotic dog loves chasing his own tail. • It is unwise to trust a liar.

> opposites: sensible • wise

simple (adjective)

If something is **simple**, it is easy to do or understand.
*Bella liked doing **simple** maths problems.*

> • easy • clear • plain

• Our chemistry teacher showed us an easy way to do the experiment.
• "The answer is clear," said the teacher. • It was plain to see who was in charge.

> opposites: complicated • difficult

sleep (verb)

When you **sleep**, you close your eyes and rest.
*Our dog loves to **sleep** on his favourite blanket.*

> • nap • snooze • doze • slumber

• The baby likes to nap in his cot. • Cats snooze whenever they can.
• Grandpa tried to doze in the sun. • Dad slumbered while we watched a film.

> opposite: awaken

93

Ss

slide (verb)

To **slide** means to move easily along a surface.
*Noah loves to **slide** in the playground.*

> • glide • skate • slip • skid

- The dancers glide across the floor.
- I love to skate at the ice rink.
- "Dad slipped on a banana skin!" giggled Suzy.
- We skid on the kitchen floor when it has been polished.

slow (adjective)

If something is **slow**, it takes a long time.
*Snails are **slow** creatures.*

> • sluggish • plodding • leisurely

- Mrs Hawkins felt sluggish after her operation. • The man walked with plodding steps.
- We took a leisurely stroll to the shop.

> opposites: fast • quick

small (adjective)

If something is **small**, it is little or tiny.
*The sparrow is a **small** garden bird.*

> • little • miniature • tiny

- The baby wore little mittens. • I bought a miniature
table for my doll's house. • A bumblebee has tiny wings.

> opposites: big • huge • large

smell (noun)

A **smell** is something that your nose detects.
*The dog picked up the **smell** of his owner.*

> • odour • scent • fragrance • aroma

- The sweaty trainers had a horrible odour.
- The candle had a scent like gingerbread.
- Flowers give off a lovely fragrance. • "What a wonderful aroma!" cried the hungry man.

smooth (adjective)

If something is **smooth**, it has no bumps or roughness.
*The winter ice rink had a **smooth** surface.*

> • glossy • polished • shiny • sleek

• I wrote my invitations on glossy paper. • Dad gave the table a polished finish.
• My sister has lovely, shiny hair. • I like to stroke my cat's sleek coat.

> opposites: coarse • rough

sorry (adjective)

If you are **sorry,** you regret something you have said or done.
*"I'm **sorry** I broke the vase," said Kitty.*

> • apologetic • ashamed • regretful • remorseful

• The waiter was apologetic about the horrible food.
• We felt ashamed that we had not believed our friend.
• I am regretful because I treated my sister badly.
• The remorseful bully asked us to forgive him.

> opposites: unapologetic • unashamed • remorseless

sort (noun)

A **sort** is a brand, a group, or a kind.
*"Guess what **sort** of cakes I've baked?" I said.*

> • type • kind • brand

• Colin likes all types of music. • We saw many kinds of bird on
our walk. • I always use the same brand of toothpaste.

spare (adjective)

If something is **spare**, it is extra or more than is needed.
*There was a **spare** seat next to me in the theatre.*

> • additional • extra • leftover

• We had five additional tickets.
• "Who would like the extra mushrooms?" asked Dad.
• There were six leftover glasses.

a
b
c
d
e
f
g
h
i
j
k
l
m
n
o
p
q
r
s
t
u
v
w
x
y
z

Ss

speak (verb)

To **speak** means to talk.
*Ian used his mobile phone to **speak** to his mum.*

> • talk • chat • converse

• You should not talk in assembly. • I can chat to my best friend about anything.
• The men were conversing loudly in the corridor.

special (adjective)

If something is **special**, it is important and unusual.
*Eliza won a very **special** prize in the competition.*

> • significant • important • unique

• Your birthday is a significant day. • "You are very important to me," Hugh said.
• The ancient vase was unique.

> opposites: common • ordinary

speed (verb)

To **speed** means to move very quickly.
*Racing cars **speed** around the track in the Grand Prix.*

> • race • hurry • rush • zoom

• Polly had to race to be on time.
• "Hurry up and get changed," said the PE teacher.
• The fans rushed to see the film star.
• We zoomed down the road on our scooters.

> opposite: crawl

spin (verb)

To **spin** means to turn around very quickly.
*I watched the laundry **spin** inside the washing machine.*

> • twirl • whirl • revolve

• Jasmine twirled to show off her new dress.
• The fallen leaves whirled in the strong wind.
• The hotel doors revolve to let people in and out.

sport (noun)

A **sport** is a physical game you play to win or to have fun.
*My brother plays **sport** three times a week.*

> • activity • exercise • pastime

- Outdoor activities such as rock climbing are great fun.
- Swimming is really good exercise.
- Their favourite pastime is gymnastics.

start (verb)

To **start** something is to begin it or make it begin.
*When he **started** the race, Jason was in the lead.*

> • begin • open • set up

- "Begin on page five," said the teacher.
- She opened the game by serving an ace.
- My cousin set up the school drama club.

> opposites: end • finish

stay (verb)

To **stay** means to remain. • *Freddie had to **stay** inside because he had a cold.*

> • remain • settle • linger

- It started to rain so we remained in the car. • The family decided to settle in Canada.
- The smell of fish lingered in the kitchen.

> opposites: go • leave

stop (verb)

To **stop** means to come to an end, or to halt.
*The police officer signalled to the vehicles to **stop**.*

> • cease • finish • halt

- The noise ceased at midnight. • I finish work at five every day.
- Charlotte skidded to a halt on her bike.

> opposite: start • go

97

a b c d e f g h i j k l m n o p q r s t u v w x y z

Ss

story (noun)

A **story** is a description of real or made-up events.
*Our teacher read us an exciting **story** yesterday.*

> • tale • account • fairy tale • legend

• Patrick did not believe his friend's tale. • I gave my account of what had happened.
• "Read me a fairy tale," begged the little girl. • We like to hear about the legend of Robin Hood.

strange (adjective)

If something is **strange**, it is odd or unusual.
*There was a **strange** smell coming from the kitchen.*

> • curious • weird • odd • peculiar

• Grandpa told us a curious story. • "Can you hear that weird noise?"
asked Harriet. • The man had an odd way of walking.
• John asked a peculiar question in class today.

> opposites: common • ordinary • usual

strict (adjective)

To be **strict** means to be severe about obeying the rules.
*Our teacher is **strict** but fair.*

> • firm • severe • stern • harsh

• The library has firm rules about how many books you can borrow. • The old lady's severe
expression scared George. • The stern coach would not let anyone talk during football practice.
• Mandy was upset by her brother's harsh words.

strong (adjective)

To be **strong** means to have great power or force.
*Cart horses are amazingly **strong.***

> • tough • stout • sturdy

• "I'm as tough as old boots!" grinned Dad.
• A swing dangled from the stout tree in our garden.
• The bike was sturdy enough to ride off-road.

> opposite: weak

stupid (adjective)

Stupid means to be unintelligent or unwise.
*It would be **stupid** to approach a python.*

> • brainless • dense • dim • foolish

- "What a brainless thing to do!" said Mum.
- Dylan is dense when it comes to history.
- Our dog is a bit dim at times. • Crossing a road from between parked cars is a foolish idea.

> opposites: clever • intelligent • smart

sudden (adjective)

Sudden means fast or unexpected. • *My **sudden** movement scared the birds.*

> • abrupt • surprising • quick • unexpected

- The ballet came to an abrupt end when the stage collapsed.
- The story had a surprising twist at the end. • The car took a quick right turn.
- An unexpected visitor arrived at the house.

> opposite: gradual

sulk (verb)

To **sulk** is to be quiet because you are angry or in a bad mood. • *"Please don't **sulk** just because you didn't win the game," said Phil.*

> • brood • mope • scowl

- Anna couldn't stop brooding about her silly mistake.
- My brother just mopes around the house all day.
- Sarah scowled when Dad didn't give her any sweets.

sure (adjective)

If something is **sure**, it is not in doubt.
*Kitty was **sure** that she had seen the man somewhere before.*

> • certain • positive • definite

- The farmer was certain that his bull had won first prize.
- Eve was positive she could pass the test. • Jack had a definite plan.

Tt

take (verb)

To **take** means to get hold of something or carry it with you.
*The bully tried to **take** Bob's sweets.*

> • seize • grasp • clutch • carry

- I seized the oars and rowed away. • "Grasp the rope tightly," shouted the climber.
- The nervous girl clutched her father's hand. • Mia carried the glass carefully.

> opposite: give

talk (verb)

To **talk** means to say words.
*Jamelia **talks** loudly when she's on the phone.*

> • chat • speak • tell

- We chatted all the way home.
- "Don't speak to anyone you don't know," said my dad.
- My best friend came over to tell me about the party.

tall (adjective)

To be **tall** means to be above average height.
*Rapunzel was kept locked in a **tall** tower.*

> • big • high • lanky • towering

- The big boys played on the football team.
- The high wall was hard to climb. • Leo was a lanky teenager.
- The towering building seemed to touch the clouds.

> opposites: low • short • small

teacher (noun)

A **teacher** is someone whose job is helping others to learn.
*Miss Brooks is our new **teacher**.*

> • instructor • tutor • professor

- I was scared of skiing, but my instructor helped me.
- Kara had a tutor to teach her advanced maths.
- "Pay attention in class!" shouted the professor.

a
b
c
d
e
f
g
h
i
j
k
l
m
n
o
p
q
r
s
t
u
v
w
x
y
z

tear (verb)

To **tear** means to rip.
*I didn't mean to **tear** my brother's book.*

> • rip • slit • split

- We ripped up old magazines for our craft project.
- The thorns slit holes in my jacket.
- Nick split the loaf of bread into four portions.

tell (verb)

To **tell** means to give information in words.
*My grandpa always **tells** good stories.*

> • announce • confess • state • notify

- Matthew and Emily announced the birth of their baby.
- The accused decided to confess the truth.
- The witness had to state how the accident happened.
- "Please notify me when you feel better," said the doctor.

temper (noun)

A **temper** is an angry mood.
*Rhinoceroses have a bad **temper**.*

> • rage • tantrum • fury

- Our teacher was in a rage because we were late.
- My naughty little brother threw a tantrum.
- Mum flew into a fury when she saw my bedroom.

thick (adjective)

To be **thick** means to be large in width or depth.
*The book was so **thick**, it took me three months to finish reading it.*

> • broad • wide • deep

- The wrestler puffed out his broad chest.
- Our new car was too wide to fit in the garage.
- We walked through the deep blanket of snow.

> opposite: thin

Tt

thin (adjective)

To be **thin** means to be small in width or depth.
*I drew an alien with **thin** arms and legs.*

> • skinny • slender • lean • slim

- The prisoner looked pale and skinny.
- A breeze shook the slender tree.
- The stray dog was scruffy and lean.
- Brian gave his girlfriend a slim book of poetry.

> opposites: fat • thick

thing (noun)

Thing is a word that describes any object that is not alive.
*"What is that **thing**?" asked Lara.*

> • article • object • item

- The shop sells all sorts of household articles. • I did not know what the stone objects in the museum were. • We donate all our unwanted items to charity.

think (verb)

To **think** means to form ideas in your mind.
*John tried hard to **think** of an answer.*

> • ponder • consider • reason • muse

- The poet sat down to ponder. • I did not consider that I was wrong. • The hikers reasoned they should go south. • "There can only be one answer," mused the detective.

throw (verb)

To **throw** means to send something through the air using your arm and hand.
*Reuben can **throw** a ball a long way.*

> • fling • hurl • toss • pitch

- I was told to fling the confetti at the bride. • "Don't hurl crayons across the room!" said Miss Frost. • The baby tossed her rattle out of the buggy. • The captain pitched a fast ball.

> opposite: catch

102

tidy (adjective)

Tidy means neat and in order. • *Dad told me to keep my bedroom **tidy**.*

> • neat • orderly • well-kept

• Alana's clothes are neat and clean. • Mr Lee has an orderly classroom.
• Lots of visitors came to see the well-kept gardens.

> opposites: messy • untidy

tight (adjective)

If something is **tight**, it fits with no room to spare.
*Amy's jacket was getting too **tight**.*

> • close-fitting • cramped • snug

• The man wore a close-fitting waistcoat. • Space was cramped in the crowded train. • Gail's shoes were a snug fit.

> opposite: loose

tiny (adjective)

If something is **tiny**, it is very small. • *I saw a **tiny** mouse on top of the cupboard.*

> • little • minute • small

• The children love their little rabbit. • Hazel was scared of the minute spider.
• The woodsman had a small cut on his hand.

> opposites: big • huge • large

tired (adjective)

If you are **tired**, you feel that you need to rest.
*Archie was so **tired** he couldn't stop yawning.*

> • exhausted • weary • worn out • sleepy

• The exhausted children went to sleep early.
• "You look weary," said Mum. • I was worn out after the race. • We were too sleepy to watch the late film.

> opposites: energetic • fresh

a b c d e f g h i j k l m n o p q r s **t** u v w x y z

Tt

top (noun)

The **top** is the highest part. • *Snow covered the **tops** of the trees.*

> • tip • crown • peak

- The explorers could see the tip of the iceberg from their boat.
- White hairs sprouted from the crown of the old man's head.
- The climber reached the mountain's peak.

> opposites: base • bottom

touch (verb)

To **touch** something means to feel it.
*You have to **touch** the button to make the lamp work.*

> • handle • feel • pat

- When I handled the vase I broke it. • Courtney reached out to feel the dress. • Mum said I could pat the dog.

tough (adjective)

To be **tough** means to be strong and sturdy.
*The tortoise's shell was **tough** and protective.*

> • hardy • brawny • sturdy

- The hardy fishermen go out in all weathers. • "I need a brawny helper to carry this box," said Miss Robson. • There is a sturdy table in our playroom.

> opposite: weak

trap (verb)

To **trap** something means to catch or hold it so that it cannot escape.
*I managed to **trap** the spider under a glass.*

> • capture • catch • corner

- The rangers tried to capture the lion.
- The runaway mouse was impossible to catch.
- The officers cornered the robbers.

> opposite: release

travel (verb)

To **travel** means to go from one place to another.
*I have to **travel** for two hours to see my uncle.*

> • go • journey • move • tour

- We go to school every day on foot.
- As Stanley journeyed north, the air became colder.
- The lorry didn't move for an hour because of roadworks.
- We toured all over South America last summer.

treasure (noun)

Treasure is something of great value or reward.
*The pirates' **treasure** was gold and jewels.*

> • wealth • fortune • riches • valuables

- "I will give away my wealth," said the generous woman.
- My new school shoes cost a small fortune.
- The road to riches is often a long one.
- Our valuables are locked away in the safe.

treat (verb)

How you **treat** someone is how you behave towards that person.
*Kyle's foster parents **treat** him well.*

> • deal with • handle • use

- "I deal with every player fairly," said the umpire. • Dr Morgan handles her patients with kindness.
- "Use the lab equipment carefully," said our teacher.

trick (verb)

To **trick** someone is to fool them or play a joke on them.
*A dishonest man **tricked** me into buying a fake diamond ring.*

> • fool • deceive • cheat • mislead

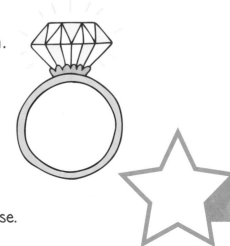

- Jennifer fooled me into thinking I had won a big prize.
- Tom deliberately tried to deceive his teacher.
- He won the card game by cheating when no one was looking.
- Dad had to mislead Mum to keep her birthday present a surprise.

true (adjective)

If something is **true**, it is real or factual.
*Everything the reporter said was **true**.*

> • correct • genuine • real

• Only I knew the correct answer. • Wesley has a genuine love of music.
• The spy told no one his real name.

> opposites: false • untrue

trust (verb)

To **trust** someone means to have confidence in them.
*The farmer **trusted** his dog to look after the sheep.*

> • believe • count on • depend on

• The shop manager believed the customer when no one else did.
• "Can I count on you to keep a secret?" asked Chloe.
• You can never depend on my sister to be on time.

> opposite: mistrust

try (verb)

To **try** something means to make an effort to do it.
*Jake would love to **try** skydiving.*

> • aim • attempt • strive

• Our team captain always aims to win. • The climbers will attempt to climb the highest peak in the mountain range. • Good competitors always strive to do their best.

turn (verb)

To **turn** means to move in a circular direction.
*Ben can **turn** the wheels on his wheelchair easily.*

> • revolve • rotate • spin • pivot

• The dancers revolved around the ballroom.
• The planets rotate around the sun.
• Some performers can spin plates on sticks.
• A ballerina can pivot on the points of her shoes.

Uu

ugly (adjective)

If something is **ugly**, it is not nice to look at. • *Toads are **ugly** creatures.*

> • hideous • unattractive

• The monster had a hideous face. • Laura wore an unattractive coat.

> opposites: beautiful • pretty

under (preposition)

If something is **under**, it is below something else.
*When it rains, I keep dry **under** my umbrella.*

> • below • beneath • underneath

• The pirate had a scar below his right eye.
• The old woman hid the dog beneath her chair.
• "Put the box underneath the table," said Miss Fox.

understand (verb)

To **understand** something is to know what it means.
*Anna could **understand** some French and Spanish.*

> • grasp • know • get

• The pilot tried to grasp the meaning of the message from the control tower.
• Tom and Todd know how aeroplanes work. • The new student did not get the joke.

> opposite: misunderstand

undo (verb)

To **undo** means to loosen or untie.
*"**Undo** your laces before you take off your shoes," said Mum.*

> • untie • open • unbutton

• Karen untied the red ribbon on her present.
• Someone had already opened the box of biscuits.
• The doctor unbuttoned his coat.

> opposites: fasten • tie

a
b
c
d
e
f
g
h
i
j
k
l
m
n
o
p
q
r
s
t
u
v
w
x
y
z

Uu

unfair (adjective)

If something is **unfair**, it is not right or equal. • *The game was **unfair** because Tim cheated.*

> • unjust • biased • one-sided • prejudiced

- The prisoner was given an unjust sentence. • The driver wrote a biased report about the accident.
- The rugby match was a one-sided affair. • Mr Jones has a prejudiced view of teenagers.

> opposites: fair • just

unhappy (adjective)

If you are **unhappy**, you feel sad. • *Rose was **unhappy** when her cat ran away.*

> • downcast • miserable • sad

- He was downcast because he did not make the team.
- The miserable woman never seemed to smile.
- The girl was sad because her best friend had moved away.

> opposites: glad • happy

unkind (adjective)

If someone is **unkind**, that person causes pain and sadness to others.
*It is **unkind** to tease shy people.*

> • cruel • nasty • mean • spiteful

- The cruel man left his dog out in the rain. • "Don't be so nasty!" sobbed Helena.
- I don't like it when people are mean to me. • Our neighbour was a spiteful person.

> opposite: kind

untidy (adjective)

If something is **untidy**, it is in a mess.
*The toy cupboard at the nursery was so **untidy**.*

> • cluttered • sloppy • messy • chaotic

- Our attic is cluttered with junk. • The boy's homework was sloppy.
- Ginny is such a messy eater! • The holiday was chaotic, but fun.

> opposites: neat • tidy

a
b
c
d
e
f
g
h
i
j
k
l
m
n
o
p
q
r
s
t
u
v
w
x
y
z

urgent (adjective)

Something **urgent** needs attention right away.
*The nurse answered an **urgent** call.*

> • important • crucial • pressing

- My parents got an important letter from the headteacher.
- It's crucial to see a doctor if you think you have appendicitis.
- The manager had to rush because she had a pressing appointment.

> opposites: unimportant • trivial

use (verb)

To **use** something means to put it into action. • *He **used** a knife to open the parcel.*

> • employ • utilize • wield

- The cafe employs ten people. • Our bodies utilize vitamins to keep us healthy.
- The knights wielded heavy swords in battle.

useful (adjective)

If something is **useful**, it helps you or has value.
*Dad bought me a **useful** present – a pencil case for school.*

> • practical • handy • helpful

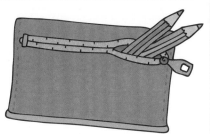

- An umbrella is practical in the rain. • Dad got some handy hints about looking after his car. • Mum thanked Gilbert for being a helpful boy.

> opposite: useless

useless (adjective)

If something is **useless**, it has no purpose or meaning.
*The hairbrush was **useless** to the bald man.*

> • pointless • worthless • futile

- It was pointless even asking for second helpings.
- The broken vase was now worthless.
- "It is futile to try to escape," said the guard.

> opposite: useful

Vv

vain (adjective)

If you are **vain**, you think too highly of yourself.
*Betty was **vain** about her appearance.*

- conceited • proud • self-important

- Bobby was conceited about his football skills.
- Mel was proud of her exam results.
- The mayor was a self-important man.

opposite: modest

vanish (verb)

To **vanish** means to disappear.
*The magician **vanished** in a puff of smoke.*

- disappear • evaporate • fade away

- The bruise on my leg disappeared after a few days. • The water evaporated in the hot sunshine.
- As she grew older, her memories began to fade away.

opposite: appear

very (adverb)

Very means to a great degree. • *The trapeze artist was **very** brave.*

- absolutely • exceedingly • extremely • particularly

- The weather outside was absolutely perfect.
- My sister works exceedingly hard at school. • Josh was extremely lucky to win the prize. • The editor wrote particularly well.

opposites: hardly • slightly

view (noun)

The **view** is what you can see from where you are.
*We had a mountain **view** from our hotel bedroom.*

- scene • vista • outlook

- The artist painted the mountain scene. • A vista of flowers lay in front of us. • "What a nice outlook!" said the guide.

a
b
c
d
e
f
g
h
i
j
k
l
m
n
o
p
q
r
s
t
u
v
w
x
y
z

violent (adjective)

To be **violent** means to use a lot of force or strength.
*A **violent** storm with strong winds and heavy rain
is called a hurricane.*

> • savage • raging • brutal

• Some breeds of dog are particularly savage.
• The raging ocean pounded the shore.
• Hockey can sometimes be a brutal game.

> opposites: calm • gentle • peaceful

visible (adjective)

If something is **visible**, it can be seen.
*The cyclist was **visible** in the driver's rear-view mirror.*

> • noticeable • clear • apparent • in view

• The batsman had a noticeable bruise on his arm.
• The seas around the tropical island were warm and clear.
• Ian's surprise was apparent on his face. • My presents were in view on the table.

visit (verb)

To **visit** means to go to see someone or something.
*Granny took me to **visit** the city art gallery.*

> • call on • go to see • look up

• "Don't forget to call on Grandpa," said Mum.
• We go to see our cousins once a year.
• The former student went to look up his old friends.

visitor (noun)

A **visitor** is someone who visits a place or person.
*The **visitors** were given a guided tour.*

> • caller • company • guest • tourist

• They had lots of callers when the baby was born. • "I enjoy having
company," said Aunt Bea. • The guests were given the best rooms.
• Every summer the city is filled with tourists.

Ww

wait (verb)

To **wait** means to stay in one place or do nothing until something happens.
*We had to **wait** fifteen minutes for the next bus.*

> • linger • loiter • remain

- The gardener did not want to linger in the cold.
- The boy loitered outside the school gate.
- I remained at the house until my friends arrived.

wake (verb)

To **wake** means to stop being asleep.
*Olivia has to **wake** at seven o'clock.*

> • rise • rouse • stir

- Most farmers have to rise before dawn.
- The lazy man did not rouse himself until lunchtime.
- Grandpa was so tired he did not stir when the alarm clock went off.

> opposite: sleep

walk (verb)

To **walk** means to move along on foot.
*Jess **walks** her dog twice a day.*

> • amble • hike • stride • stroll

- The man ambled along the road. • The family hikes five miles every Sunday. • My dad came striding across the room.
- "Let's go for a stroll," suggested Theo.

wander (verb)

To **wander** means to move around with no purpose.
*A sheep **wandered** into our garden!*

> • roam • meander • drift • rove

- The traveller had roamed all over Europe.
- Zack and I meandered through the fairground.
- The lonely boy drifted around the city centre.
- The hunters roved through the forest.

want (verb)

To **want** something means to wish to have it.
*She **wants** a new dress for the school disco.*

> • desire • crave • long for

• The genie offered Aladdin whatever he desired. • Liz was craving something sweet to eat.
• The wet campers longed for a sunny day.

warm (adjective)

If something is **warm**, it is of medium heat.
*My winter coat keeps me nice and **warm**.*

> • balmy • heated • tepid

• It was such a balmy day that we decided to sit outside.
• The outdoor swimming pool was heated.
• Ella washed her woollen sweater in tepid water.

> opposite: cool

wash (verb)

To **wash** something means to clean it with water.
*Willow **washed** her muddy hands under the tap.*

> • bathe • clean • launder • rinse

• I love to bathe in a bubble bath. • Dad decided to clean the fish tank.
• You can launder clothes at a launderette. • I rinsed out the bath
after washing our smelly dog.

waste (verb)

To **waste** something means to use it up carelessly.
*The governor told people not to **waste** water.*

> • throw away • fritter away • squander

• The boys throw away their money on silly games.
• "Don't fritter away your pocket money," said Dad.
• Tamara squandered her time at school.

> opposite: save

a b c d e f g h i j k l m n o p q r s t u v w x y z

Ww

watch (verb)

To **watch** something means to look at it.
*We **watched** the play from the front row.*

> • observe • view • stare at • gaze

- Daniel observed some rare birds in the park.
- I viewed the match from behind the goal.
- "Don't stare at me," said the injured boy. • I saw a large tanker as I gazed out to sea.

wave (verb)

To **wave** means to move from side to side or up and down.
*Dad **waved** goodbye before leaving for work.*

> • flutter • flap • sway

- Butterflies flutter their wings.
- The pigeon flapped its wings when I approached it.
- The young trees swayed in the storm.

way (noun)

A **way** of doing something is a method of doing it.
*There are many different **ways** to cook eggs.*

> • method • manner • fashion

- My brother taught me a new method of tying my shoelaces.
- The saleswoman spoke to me in a rude manner.
- The work was completed in a casual fashion.

weak (adjective)

Something or someone that is **weak** has very little strength.
*"I am not as **weak** as I look!" said Timmy.*

> • feeble • delicate • frail • puny

- The sick man was too feeble to get out of bed.
- Cups made of bone china are very delicate.
- The frail old man walked with a cane.
- His legs were muscly, but his arms were puny!

opposite: strong

weird (adjective)

If something is **weird**, it is strange or unusual.
*It would be **weird** to see a unicorn at the zoo!*

> • strange • odd • peculiar • unusual

• I saw a strange shadow in the doorway. • Jane thought it was odd when her friend forgot her birthday. • The green smoothie tasted peculiar. • The film star wore unusual clothes.

> opposites: usual • normal

welcome (adjective)

If something is **welcome**, it is received gladly.
*The hotel owner makes all his guests feel **welcome**.*

> • acceptable • wanted • pleasant

• "This is an acceptable idea," said Professor Lau. • Our new kitten is a wanted addition to our home. • I got a pleasant surprise in the post today.

> opposites: unwanted • unwelcome

well (adjective)

If you are **well**, you are healthy. • *The doctor said I was fit and **well**.*

> • fit • thriving • healthy

• Olympic athletes have to be very fit. • "Your dog is thriving," said the vet.
• Being out in the fresh air makes you feel healthy.

> opposites: ill • sick • poorly • unwell

well (adverb)

If something is done **well**, it is done in a good way. • *The thriller was **well** written.*

> • agreeably • acceptably • properly

• The students promised to behave agreeably. • "You have done your work acceptably," said Mr Dixon. • The tour guide liked to do her job properly.

> opposite: badly

Ww

wet (adjective)

To be **wet** means to be covered with liquid. • *Our kitten doesn't like getting **wet**.*

> • moist • soggy • soaking • sopping

• The dog's nose was moist. • I pulled the soggy book out of the water. • "You're soaking!" cried Mum when I came in from the rain. • He put the sopping clothes into the dryer.

> opposite: dry

whole (adjective)

If something is **whole** it has nothing left out. • *The recipe called for six **whole** eggs.*

> • entire • total • full • complete

• "I have finished the entire book," boasted my sister. • The cashier wanted the total amount. • I wanted Dad to hear the full story. • We spent an hour in complete silence.

> opposite: partial

wicked (adjective)

To be **wicked** means to be very bad. • *The **wicked** witch mixed up a potion.*

> • heartless • fiendish • evil

• A heartless thief stole the old man's life savings. • The fiendish pirate attacked the ship. • The cruel dictator had an evil plan.

> opposites: good • harmless

wide (adjective)

If something is **wide** it measures a long way from one side to the other. • *The tree trunk was so **wide**, I could not reach around it.*

> • large • broad • vast

• The dog escaped through a large gap in the fence. • The giant had broad shoulders. • The fleet of ships sailed down the vast river.

> opposite: narrow

wild (adjective)

If something is **wild**, it lives freely.
*In the nature reserve we saw lots of **wild** animals.*

> • untamed • feral • free

- The untamed horse could not be ridden. • There is a feral cat living in the woods.
- I wanted the circus animals to be free.

> opposite: tame

win (verb)

To **win** means to finish first in a game or competition.
*Debbie was pleased to **win** the fun run.*

> • triumph • come in first • succeed

- The girls' team triumphed in the netball competition.
- Jamie came in first in the 100-metre sprint.
- Samuel succeeded in beating last year's winner.

> opposite: lose

wind (verb)

To **wind** something means to turn or coil it.
*Dad **winds** the hose up after he has used it.*

> • bend • twist • curve

- I tried to bend the wire around my finger. • The climber twisted the rope around his waist.
- "The road curves to the left," said the driver.

> opposite: straighten

woods (noun)

Woods consist of a large group of trees.
*We went for a stroll in the **woods**.*

> • forest • copse • grove

- "I found some acorns in the forest," said Nat.
- The copse is our favourite place. • Big apple trees grow in the grove.

a b c d e f g h i j k l m n o p q r s t u v w x y z

work (noun)

Work is physical or mental effort.
The delivery man had lots of work to do.

> • labour • toil • effort

- Building houses takes a lot of labour.
- Ruben's toil was rewarded with praise.
- "Please make an effort to behave!" said Mum.

> opposites: play • rest

worry (verb)

To **worry** means to feel concerned. • *We all started to worry about the weather.*

> • fret • agonize • be anxious

- We tried not to fret about the missing costumes.
- I agonized over whether to tell my best friend a secret.
- "Try not to be so anxious," said the kind nurse.

write (verb)

To **write** means to form words with a pen
or pencil, or to create something with words.
The English students had to write a story.

> • compose • jot down • scribble

- Daryl tried to compose a thank-you letter.
- Mum said she would jot down a shopping list.
- We had to scribble some notes in our notebooks.

wrong (adjective)

If something is **wrong** it is not correct.
I knew I had written the wrong answer.

> • mistaken • in error • incorrect

- The cashier said that he had been mistaken. • "This was done in error," said Uncle Pete.
- I gave an incorrect answer in our class quiz.

> opposites: correct • right

Yy

yell (verb)

To **yell** means to shout loudly.
*Our football coach **yells** instructions from the sidelines.*

> • bawl • bellow • scream • screech

- Babies bawl loudly if they get upset.
- The teacher bellowed at the noisy children.
- He screamed throughout the rollercoaster ride.
- "Fetch me my slippers!" screeched the pampered princess.

> opposite: whisper

young (adjective)

If you are **young** you have only been alive for a short time.
*Tammy was too **young** to go to school.*

> • youthful • growing • immature

- My dad is middle-aged but he keeps fit and feels youthful.
- "I'm a growing boy!" smiled Dylan.
- The immature bird had not yet learned to fly.

> opposite: old

Zz

zero (noun)

Zero is nothing at all.
*Dan got a score of **zero** in his science test.*

> • nothing • nil• naught

- There nothing at all in the room.
- The home team's score was nil.
- My plans for an expensive holiday came to naught.

a b c d e f g h i j k l m n o p q r s t u v w x y z

Index

All the headwords and synonyms that appear in the thesaurus are listed in alphabetical order in this index. When you find a word in the alphabetical list, the headword entry you need to look up is given after the word 'see'. For some words, there is more than one headword to look up, for example 'admire'. Where a word or headword is listed more than once, to help you find the right word the different meanings or the parts of speech are given in brackets afterwards: for example, **bad** (naughty) and **bad** (rotten) or **end** (noun) and **end** (verb).

blaze *see* BURN
blend *see* MIX
blissful *see* HAPPY
blue *see* SAD
blunder *see* MISTAKE
boast *see* BOAST
boastful *see* PROUD
boisterous *see* EXCITED
bold *see* BRAVE
boring *see* BORING
bother *see* ANNOY
bottom (backside) *see* BOTTOM
bottom (base) *see* BOTTOM
bounce *see* JUMP
brag *see* BOAST
brain *see* MIND
brainless *see* STUPID
brainy *see* BRIGHT
brand *see* SORT
brave *see* BRAVE
brawl *see* FIGHT
brawny *see* TOUGH
break (noun) *see* BREAK (noun), REST
break (verb) *see* BREAK (verb)
breed *see* KIND (noun)
bright (brainy) *see* BRIGHT
bright (shiny) *see* BRIGHT
brilliant *see* BRIGHT
bring *see* BRING, DRAW
brisk *see* QUICK
broad *see* THICK, WIDE
brood *see* SULK
bruise *see* HURT
brutal *see* CRUEL, VIOLENT
build *see* BUILD, MAKE
bump *see* JOLT
bumpy *see* ROUGH
burn *see* BURN
burning *see* HOT
burrow *see* DIG
bury *see* BURY
bustling *see* BUSY
busy *see* BUSY
bum *see* BOTTOM

C

calamity *see* DISASTER
calculate *see* COUNT
call (announce) *see* CALL
call on *see* VISIT
calm *see* CALM
calm down *see* RELAX
capable *see* ABLE
capture *see* CATCH, TRAP
care *see* CARE
careless *see* LAZY
carry *see* BRING, CARRY, HOLD, MOVE
carry out *see* DO
carve *see* CUT
cash *see* MONEY
catastrophe *see* DISASTER
catch *see* CATCH, TRAP

cease *see* END (verb), STOP
celebrated *see* FAMOUS
centre *see* MIDDLE
certain *see* CERTAIN, SURE
chain *see* ROW
chance *see* RISK
change *see* CHANGE, MONEY
changed *see* DIFFERENT
chaos *see* MESS
chaotic *see* UNTIDY
charge *see* ORDER
charming *see* BEAUTIFUL, NICE
chase *see* CHASE, FOLLOW
chat *see* SPEAK, TALK
cheap *see* CHEAP
cheat *see* TRICK
check *see* CHECK
chew *see* EAT
chief *see* MAIN
child *see* BABY, CHILD
chilly *see* COLD
choose *see* CHOOSE, DECIDE, PICK
chop *see* CUT
chore *see* JOB
chortle *see* LAUGH
chubby *see* FAT
chuckle *see* LAUGH
chunk *see* PIECE
circular *see* ROUND
clamber *see* CLIMB
clarify *see* EXPLAIN
clasp *see* HOLD
clean *see* CLEAN, CLEAR, WASH
clear (clean) *see* CLEAR
clear (plain) *see* CLEAR, EASY, SIMPLE
clever *see* BRIGHT, CLEVER
climb *see* CLIMB
clip *see* CUT
close (adj) *see* NEAR
close-fitting *see* TIGHT
closing *see* LAST (adj)
clutch *see* TAKE
clutter *see* MESS
cluttered *see* UNTIDY
cold *see* COLD
collect *see* COLLECT
collision *see* ACCIDENT
colour *see* COLOUR
colossal *see* LARGE
column *see* ROW
combine *see* MIX
come *see* COME
come about *see* HAPPEN
come first *see* WIN
come into view *see* APPEAR
come to light *see* APPEAR
comfortable *see* COSY
comical *see* FUNNY
command *see* ORDER
companion *see* FRIEND
comparable to *see* LIKE (adj)
compassionate *see* KIND (adj)

compel *see* MAKE
competition *see* MATCH
complete *see* DO, WHOLE
completed *see* OVER
completely *see* QUITE
complication *see* PROBLEM
complimentary *see* FREE
compose *see* WRITE
comprise *see* CONTAIN
conceal *see* BURY, HIDE
concealed *see* SECRET
conceited *see* VAIN
concept *see* IDEA
conclude *see* DECIDE, END (verb), FINISH
concluding *see* LAST (adj)
conclusion *see* END (noun)
concur *see* AGREE
conduct *see* BEHAVE, LEAD
confess *see* ADMIT, TELL
confident *see* CERTAIN
congregate *see* MEET
connect *see* JOIN
consider *see* THINK
considerate *see* KIND (adj)
consist *see* CONTAIN
construct *see* BUILD
consume *see* EAT
contain *see* CONTAIN
contented *see* HAPPY
contest *see* MATCH
continue *see* LAST (verb)
contrasting *see* DIFFERENT
control *see* RULE (verb)
converse *see* SPEAK
cook *see* BAKE, COOK
coordinate *see* ORGANIZE
copse *see* WOODS
core *see* MIDDLE
corner *see* TRAP
correct *see* RIGHT, TRUE
cosy *see* COSY
count *see* COUNT
count on *see* TRUST
countless *see* MANY
cover *see* BURY
cover up *see* HIDE
crack *see* BREAK (verb)
cradle *see* HOLD
craggy *see* ROUGH
cram *see* FILL
cramped *see* TIGHT
crash *see* ACCIDENT
crave *see* LONG (verb), NEED, WANT
create *see* MAKE
creature *see* CREATURE
crisp *see* CRISP
cross *see* ANGRY, CROSS
crow *see* BOAST
crown *see* TOP
cruel *see* CRUEL, MEAN, UNKIND
crunchy *see* CRISP
cry *see* CALL

cure *see* HEAL
curious *see* STRANGE
curt *see* RUDE
curve *see* BEND (verb), WIND
curved *see* ROUND
cut *see* CUT
cutting *see* SHARP

D

damage *see* DAMAGE, HARM
danger *see* DANGER, RISK
dangerous *see* FIERCE
daring *see* BRAVE
dark *see* DARK
dart *see* RUN
dash *see* HURRY, RUN
dazzling *see* BRIGHT
deafening *see* LOUD, NOISY
deal with *see* TREAT
deceive *see* TRICK
decide *see* DECIDE
decide on *see* PICK
decline *see* REFUSE
decree *see* RULE (noun)
deep *see* THICK
defend *see* PROTECT
definite *see* SURE
delayed *see* LATE
delicate *see* WEAK
delicious *see* DELICIOUS
delighted *see* GLAD, HAPPY
demanding *see* HARD
demolish *see* DESTROY, RUIN
demonstrate *see* EXPLAIN
dense *see* STUPID
deny *see* REFUSE
depart *see* GO (verb), LEAVE
depend on *see* TRUST
descend *see* FALL
desire *see* LONG (verb), WANT
despise *see* HATE
destitute *see* POOR
destroy *see* DAMAGE, DESTROY, RUIN
detect *see* DISCOVER, NOTICE
determine *see* DECIDE
detest *see* HATE
devastate *see* DAMAGE
develop *see* GROW
different *see* DIFFERENT
difficult *see* HARD
dig *see* DIG
dignified *see* GRAND
dim *see* DARK, STUPID
direct *see* ORDER
dirty *see* DIRTY
disagree *see* ARGUE
disappear *see* VANISH
disaster *see* ACCIDENT, DISASTER
discover *see* DISCOVER, FIND
dislike *see* HATE
dismal *see* UNHAPPY
disobedient *see* NAUGHTY

dispatch *see* SEND
display *see* SHOW
displeased *see* ANGRY
dissolve *see* MELT
distribute *see* SHARE
dive *see* FALL
divide *see* SHARE
do *see* DO
dodge *see* MISS
donate *see* GIVE
doodle *see* DRAW (sketch)
dote on *see* LOVE
doubt *see* DOUBT
downcast *see* UNHAPPY
downpour *see* RAIN
doze *see* SLEEP
drag *see* PULL
draw (attract) *see* DRAW
draw (sketch) *see* DRAW
dread *see* FEAR
dreadful *see* HORRIBLE
dreary *see* BORING
drizzle *see* RAIN
drop by *see* CALL
drop *see* FALL, LOSE (verb)
dry *see* DRY
dull (boring) *see* BORING

E

eager *see* EAGER, KEEN
earlier *see* OLD, IDEAL
earn *see* GET
earth *see* LAND (noun)
easy *see* EASY, SIMPLE
eat *see* EAT
edgy *see* NERVOUS
effort *see* GO (noun), WORK
elderly *see* OLD
elect *see* CHOOSE
elevate *see* RAISE
elsewhere *see* OUT
eminent *see* FAMOUS
employ *see* USE
empty *see* EMPTY
end (noun) *see* END (noun)
end (verb) *see* END (verb), FINISH
ended *see* OVER
ending *see* END (noun)
endless *see* LONG (adj)
endure *see* LAST (verb)
energetic *see* ACTIVE
enigma *see* MYSTERY
enjoy *see* ENJOY, LIKE (verb)
enjoyable *see* AMUSING
enormous *see* BIG, ENORMOUS,
enough *see* ENOUGH
enquire *see* ASK
ensemble *see* BAND
entertaining *see* FUNNY
enthusiastic *see* EAGER, KEEN
entice *see* DRAW (attract)
entire *see* WHOLE

envious *see* JEALOUS
equal *see* EVEN, FAIR
error *see* MISTAKE
escalate *see* RAISE
escort *see* LEAD
estimate *see* GUESS
evade *see* MISS
evaluate *see* JUDGE
evaporate *see* VANISH
even (flat) *see* EVEN
even (the same) *see* EVEN
everyday *see* ORDINARY
evil *see* BAD, EVIL, WICKED
exact *see* PERFECT, RIGHT
examine *see* CHECK, LOOK
excavate *see* DIG
exceedingly *see* VERY
excellent *see* EXCELLENT, GOOD
excited *see* EXCITED
exclaim *see* SAY
excursion *see* JOURNEY
execute *see* KILL
exhausted *see* TIRED
expedition *see* JOURNEY
explain *see* EXPLAIN
exquisite *see* LOVELY
extended *see* LONG (adj)
extra *see* SPARE
extraordinary *see* EXTRAORDINARY,
  FANTASTIC
extremely *see* VERY

F

fade away *see* VANISH
fair *see* FAIR
fairy tale *see* STORY
fall *see* FALL
famished *see* HUNGRY
famous *see* FAMOUS
fantastic *see* FANTASTIC
far-fetched *see* FANTASTIC, INCREDIBLE
fashion *see* WAY
fast *see* FAST, QUICK
fat *see* FAT
faultless *see* IDEAL, PERFECT
fear *see* FEAR
fearful *see* AFRAID
fearless *see* BRAVE
feast *see* MEAL
feeble *see* WEAK
feel *see* FEEL, TOUCH
feral *see* WILD
ferocious *see* FIERCE
fetch *see* BRING
fiendish *see* WICKED
fierce *see* FIERCE
fight *see* FIGHT
fill *see* FILL
filthy *see* DIRTY
final *see* LAST (adj)
find *see* DISCOVER, FIND
fine *see* BEAUTIFUL, HANDSOME

finger see FEEL
finish see END (noun), END (verb), FINISH, STOP
finished see OVER
firm see CRISP, HARD, STRICT
first class see GOOD
fit see WELL (adj)
fitter see BETTER
fix see FIX, MEND
flame see BURN
flap see WAVE
flare see BURN
flat see EVEN
flawless see PERFECT
fling see THROW
float see FLY
flutter see WAVE
fly see FLY, RUSH
follow see FOLLOW
following see NEXT
food see FOOD
fool see TRICK
foolish see SILLY, STUPID
foot see BOTTOM
force see MAKE
forest see WOODS
forget see FORGET
former see OLD
formerly see ONCE
forsaken see LONELY
fortune see TREASURE
forward see SEND
fracture see BREAK (verb)
fragment see PART
fragrance see SMELL
frail see WEAK
free see FREE, RESCUE, WILD
free (available) see FREE
free (complimentary) see FREE
freezing see COLD
frequently see OFTEN
fresh see CLEAN, NEW
fret see WORRY
friend see FRIEND
friendless see LONELY
fright see FEAR
frighten see FRIGHTEN
frightened see AFRAID
fritter away see WASTE
frolic see PLAY
frosty see COLD
fully grown see ADULT
fully see QUITE
funds see MONEY
funny (amusing) see AMUSING, FUNNY
funny (odd) see FUNNY
furious see ANGRY, MAD
fury see TEMPER
futile see USELESS

G

gag see JOKE
gamble see RISK
game see MATCH
gap see BREAK (noun)
gaping see OPEN (adj)
gather see COLLECT, MEET
gaze see LOOK, WATCH
gentle see GENTLE, KIND (adj), MILD
genuine see REAL, TRUE
get see GET, UNDERSTAND
get along see AGREE
giant see ENORMOUS
gigantic see ENORMOUS
giggle see LAUGH
give see GIVE, PASS
glad see GLAD
gladden see PLEASE
glaring see BRIGHT
gleam see SHINE
glide see FLY, SLIDE
glimpse see SEE
glitter see SHINE
gloat see BOAST
gloomy see DARK
glorious see GRAND
glossy see SMOOTH
gluttonous see GREEDY
go (noun) see GO (noun)
go (verb) see GO (verb), LEAVE
go by see PASS
go to see see VISIT (verb)
go up see CLIMB
goal see OBJECT
gone see ABSENT
good (excellent) see GOOD
good (well behaved) see GOOD
good-looking see HANDSOME
gorgeous see PRETTY
govern see RULE (verb)
grab see GRAB
grand see GRAND
grant see GIVE
grapple see FIGHT
grasp see HOLD, TAKE, UNDERSTAND
grave see SERIOUS
great see GREAT
greedy see GREEDY, SELFISH
green with envy see JEALOUS
grimy see DIRTY
groan see MOAN
ground see LAND (noun)
grove see WOODS
group see BAND
grow see GROW
grown-up see ADULT
grubby see DIRTY
grumpy see CROSS
guard see PROTECT
guess see GUESS
guffaw see LAUGH
guide see LEAD

H

halt see STOP
hand see PASS
handle see TOUCH, TREAT
handsome see HANDSOME
handy see USEFUL
happen see HAPPEN
happy see HAPPY, GLAD
hard (rigid) see CRISP, HARD
hard (tough) see HARD
hardy see TOUGH
harm see HARM, HURT
harsh see STRICT
hasten see HURRY
hat see HAT
hate see HATE
hateful see EVIL
haul see PULL
have see HAVE
have fun see PLAY
hazard see DANGER, RISK
head see MAIN
heal see HEAL
healthy see WELL (adj)
heart see MIDDLE
heartless see CRUEL, WICKED
heat see BAKE, COOK
heated see WARM
heavy see HEAVY
hefty see HEAVY
help see HELP
helpful see USEFUL
hesitate see DOUBT
hidden see SECRET
hide see BURY, HIDE
hideous see UGLY
high see HIGH, TALL
high-ranking see IMPORTANT
hike see WALK
hilarious see AMUSING, FUNNY
hit see HIT
hoard see SAVE
hold see CONTAIN, HAVE, HOLD
hold on to see SAVE
hollow see EMPTY
honest see REAL
hop see JUMP
hopeless see IMPOSSIBLE
horrible see AWFUL, HORRIBLE
hot see HOT
hue see COLOUR
huge see BIG, ENORMOUS
hunger see LONG (verb)
hungry see HUNGRY
hunt see CHASE
hurl see THROW
hurry see HURRY, RUSH, SPEED
hurt see HARM, HURT
hushed see QUIET

I

icy *see* COLD
idea *see* IDEA
ideal *see* IDEAL
identical *see* SAME
identical to *see* LIKE (adj)
identify *see* KNOW
idiotic *see* SILLY
idle *see* LAZY
ignore *see* FORGET
ill *see* ILL
immature *see* YOUNG
immense *see* BIG, GREAT
impatient *see* EAGER
impish *see* NAUGHTY
implausible *see* INCREDIBLE
imply *see* MEAN (verb)
important *see* IMPORTANT, SPECIAL,
    URGENT
impossible *see* IMPOSSIBLE
impressive *see* GRAND
improved *see* GRAND
in error *see* WRONG
include *see* CONTAIN
incorrect *see* WRONG
increase *see* GROW
incredible *see* FANTASTIC, INCREDIBLE
indicate *see* MEAN (verb)
indolent *see* LAZY
inexpensive *see* CHEAP
infant *see* BABY, CHILD
ingenious *see* CLEVER
injure *see* HARM, HURT
inspect *see* CHECK
instruct *see* ORDER
instructor *see* TEACHER
insulting *see* RUDE
intellect *see* MIND
intelligence *see* MIND
intelligent *see* BRIGHT
intermission *see* BREAK (noun)
interrogate *see* ASK, QUESTION
irate *see* MAD
irritate *see* ANNOY
irritated *see* CROSS
irritation *see* NUISANCE
isolated *see* LONELY
issue *see* MATTER
item *see* OBJECT, THING

J

jealous *see* JEALOUS
jerk *see* JOLT
jest *see* JOKE
job *see* JOB
join *see* JOIN
joke *see* JOKE
jolt *see* JOLT
jot down *see* WRITE
journey *see* JOURNEY
joyful *see* GLAD
judge *see* JUDGE

jumble *see* MESS
jump *see* JUMP
just *see* FAIR, ONLY (adv)

K

keen *see* EAGER, KEEN, SHARP
keep *see* KEEP, SAVE
key *see* IMPORTANT
kid *see* CHILD
kill *see* KILL
kind (adj) *see* KIND (adj)
kind (noun) *see* KIND (noun)
knock down *see* DESTROY
knot *see* KNOT
know (identify) *see* KNOW
know (realize) *see* KNOW,
    UNDERSTAND

L

labour *see* WORK
land (noun) *see* LAND (noun)
land (verb) *see* LAND (verb)
lanky *see* TALL
large *see* BIG, LARGE, WIDE
last (adj) *see* LAST (adj)
last (verb) *see* LAST (verb)
late *see* LATE
look *see* LOOK
later *see* NEXT
laugh *see* LAUGH
launder *see* WASH
law *see* RULE (noun)
lay *see* PLACE (verb)
laze *see* RELAX
lazy *see* LAZY
lead *see* LEAD, RULE
leading *see* IMPORTANT
lean *see* THIN
leap *see* JUMP
leave *see* LEAVE, GO (verb)
leftover *see* SPARE
legend *see* STORY
leisurely *see* SLOW
lengthy *see* LONG (adj)
level *see* EVEN
lie *see* LIE
lift *see* RAISE
like (adj) *see* LIKE (adj)
like (verb) *see* ENJOY, LIKE (verb)
line *see* ROW
linger *see* STAY, WAIT
link *see* JOIN
litter *see* RUBBISH
little *see* LITTLE, SHORT, SMALL,
lively *see* ACTIVE, EXCITED
load *see* FILL
location *see* PLACE (noun)
lofty *see* HIGH
loiter *see* WAIT
lone *see* ONLY (adj)
lonely *see* LONELY
long (adj) *see* LONG (adj)

long (verb) *see* LONG (verb)
long for *see* MISS, WANT
long-faced *see* SERIOUS
look up *see* VISIT (verb)
loom *see* APPEAR
loop *see* KNOT
lose *see* LOSE
lots *see* MANY
loud *see* LOUD, NOISY
lounge *see* LIE
love *see* ENJOY, LOVE
lovely *see* BEAUTIFUL, LOVELY, PRETTY
loving *see* KIND (adj)

M

mad *see* MAD
main *see* MAIN
majestic *see* GRAND
make (compel) *see* MAKE
make (create) *see* BUILD, COOK, MAKE
make clear *see* EXPLAIN
make tracks *see* LEAVE
manner *see* WAY
many *see* MANY
mark *see* MARK
massive *see* ENORMOUS, HEAVY, LARGE
match *see* MATCH SORT
matching *see* SAME
matter *see* MATTER
mature *see* ADULT
meal *see* MEAL
mean (adj) *see* MEAN (adj),
mean (verb) *see* MEAN (verb)
meek *see* SHY
meet *see* MEET
melt *see* MELT
mend *see* FIX, HEAL, MEND
merely *see* ONLY (adv)
merge *see* MIX
mess *see* MESS
messy *see* UNTIDY
method *see* WAY
middle *see* MIDDLE
mild *see* GENTLE, MILD
mind *see* CARE, MIND
mingle *see* MIX
miniature *see* LITTLE, SMALL
minute *see* LITTLE, TINY
miserable *see* SAD, UNHAPPY
mislay *see* LOSE
misplace *see* LOSE
miss (avoid) *see* MISS
miss (pine) *see* MISS
missing *see* ABSENT
mistake *see* MISTAKE
mistaken *see* WRONG
mistrust *see* DOUBT
mix *see* MIX
moan *see* MOAN
model *see* IDEAL
modify *see* CHANGE
moist *see* WET

money *see* MONEY
monster *see* MONSTER
mope *see* SULK
mouldy *see* BAD
mound *see* PILE
mountain *see* PILE
move *see* CARRY, MOVE
much *see* OFTEN
muddy *see* DIRTY
munch *see* EAT
murder *see* KILL
murky *see* DARK
muse *see* THINK
mystery *see* MYSTERY

N

naked *see* BARE
nap *see* REST, SLEEP
narrow *see* NARROW
nasty *see* HORRIBLE, MEAN, NASTY,
   UNKIND
naughty *see* BAD, NAUGHTY
near *see* NEAR
nearly *see* ABOUT
neat *see* NEAT, TIDY
need *see* NEED
needy *see* POOR
neighbouring *see* NEAR
nervous *see* NERVOUS
new *see* NEW
newborn *see* BABY
next *see* NEXT
nice *see* NICE
noiseless *see* QUIET, SILENT
noisy *see* LOUD, NOISY
normal *see* NORMAL, ORDINARY
nosy *see* NOSY
nothing *see* ZERO
notice (verb) *see* FIND, NOTICE (verb)
notify *see* TELL
novel *see* NEW
nude *see* BARE
nuisance *see* NUISANCE
numerous *see* MANY

O

outing *see* VISIT (noun)
obedient *see* GOOD
object (aim) *see* OBJECT
object (article) *see* OBJECT, THING
oblige *see* MAKE
observant *see* ALERT
observe *see* NOTICE (verb), WATCH
obtain *see* GET
obvious *see* CLEAR
occupation *see* JOB
occupied *see* BUSY
occur *see* HAPPEN
odd *see* FUNNY, ODD, STRANGE,
   WEIRD
odour *see* SMELL
often *see* OFTEN

old (aged) *see* OLD
old (earlier) *see* OLD
omit *see* FORGET
on the house *see* FREE
on top of *see* ABOVE
once *see* ONCE
one-sided *see* UNFAIR
only (adj) *see* ONLY (adj)
only (adv) *see* ONLY (adv)
open (adj) *see* OPEN (adj)
open (verb) *see* OPEN (verb), START,
   UNDO
opening *see* START
opposite *see* DIFFERENT
opt for *see* PICK
orchestra *see* BAND
order *see* ORDER
orderly *see* NEAT, TIDY
ordinary *see* NORMAL, ORDINARY
organize *see* ARRANGE, ORGANIZE
original *see* NEW
out *see* OUT
out of the question *see* IMPOSSIBLE
outdo *see* PASS
outlook *see* VIEW
outstanding *see* EXCELLENT
outstrip *see* PASS
over *see* ABOVE, OVER
overdue *see* LATE
overlook *see* FORGET
oversight *see* MISTAKE
overweight *see* FAT
own *see* HAVE
own up *see* ADMIT

P

pack *see* FILL
painful *see* PAINFUL
pal *see* FRIEND
parched *see* DRY
part *see* PART
particularly *see* VERY
pass (give) *see* PASS
pass (go by) *see* PASS
pat *see* TOUCH
patch *see* FIX
pause *see* BREAK (noun)
peaceful *see* CALM, PEACEFUL
peak *see* TOP
peculiar *see* FUNNY, ODD, STRANGE,
   WEIRD
penniless *see* POOR
perfect *see* IDEAL, PERFECT
perform *see* DO
performer *see* ACTOR
peril *see* DANGER
persist *see* LAST (verb)
pest *see* NUISANCE
pester *see* ANNOY
pet *see* FEEL
pick *see* CHOOSE, PICK
piece *see* PART, PIECE

piercing *see* NOISY
pile *see* PILE
pine *see* MISS
pitch *see* THROW
pivot *see* TURN
place (noun) *see* PLACE (noun)
place (verb) *see* PLACE (verb)
plain *see* CLEAR, EASY, SIMPLE
plan *see* ARRANGE, IDEA
play *see* PLAY
player *see* ACTOR
pleasant *see* MILD, NICE, WELCOME
please *see* PLEASE
pleased *see* GLAD, PROUD
plodding *see* SLOW
pluck *see* GRAB
plucky *see* BRAVE
plump *see* FAT
plunge *see* FALL
pointless *see* USELESS
pointy *see* SHARP
polished *see* SMOOTH
polite *see* GOOD
ponder *see* THINK
poor *see* POOR
portion *see* PART
position *see* PLACE (noun)
positive *see* CERTAIN, SURE
possess *see* HAVE
post *see* SEND
practical *see* SENSIBLE, USEFUL
praise *see* ADMIRE
prank *see* JOKE
precise *see* RIGHT
preferable *see* BETTER
prejudiced *see* UNFAIR
prepare *see* ARRANGE, COOK
prepared *see* READY
present *see* GIVE, SHOW
press *see* PUSH
pretty *see* PRETTY
previous *see* OLD
previously *see* ONCE
prime *see* MAIN
primed *see* READY
principal *see* MAIN
private *see* SECRET
problem *see* PROBLEM
produce *see* MAKE
professor *see* TEACHER
properly *see* WELL (adv)
protect *see* PROTECT
protected *see* SAFE
proud *see* PROUD, VAIN
provide *see* GIVE
prying *see* NOSY
pull *see* PULL
pull in *see* DRAW
punch *see* HIT
puny *see* WEAK
pure *see* CLEAR
purpose *see* OBJECT

pursue see CHASE, FOLLOW
push see MOVE, PUSH
put see PLACE (verb)
puzzle see MYSTERY

Q

quarrel see ARGUE
queasy see ILL
query see ASK
question see DOUBT, QUESTION
quick see FAST, QUICK, SUDDEN
quick-witted see CLEVER
quiver see SHAKE
quiz see QUESTION
quiet see CALM, PEACEFUL, QUIET, SILENT
quite see QUITE

R

race see SPEED
rage see TEMPER
raging see MAD, VIOLENT
rain see RAIN
raise see RAISE
rapid see FAST, QUICK
ravenous see HUNGRY
reach see COME
react see BEHAVE
ready see READY
real see REAL, TRUE
realize see KNOW
rear see BOTTOM
reason see THINK
reasonable see CHEAP, SENSIBLE
recall see REMEMBER
receive see GET
recline see LIE
recognize see KNOW
recollect see REMEMBER
recovered see BETTER
reduced see CHEAP
refuse see REFUSE
regretful see SORRY
regular see NORMAL, ORDINARY
regulation see RULE (noun)
relax see RELAX
remain see STAY, WAIT
remainder see REST
remark see SAY
remember see KNOW, REMEMBER
remorseful see SORRY
repair see FIX, MEND
repeatedly see OFTEN
reply see ANSWER
request see ASK
require see NEED
rescue see RESCUE
resentful see JEALOUS
reserve see KEEP
resolve see DECIDE
respect see RESPECT
respond see ANSWER
rest (nap) see BREAK (noun), RELAX, REST

rest (remainder) see REST
restful see PEACEFUL
retain see KEEP
retort see ANSWER
reveal see SHOW
revere see RESPECT
revolve see SPIN, TURN
rich see RICH
riches see MONEY
riddle see MYSTERY
right see FAIR, RIGHT
rigid see HARD
ring see BAND
rinse see WASH
rip see TEAR
rise see WAKE
risk see DANGER, RISK
roar see SHOUT
roast see BAKE
romp see PLAY
rotate see TURN
rotten see BAD
rough see ROUGH
roughly see ABOUT
round see ROUND
rouse see WAKE
row see ROW
rubbish see RUBBISH
rude see RUDE
ruin see DAMAGE, DESTROY, HARM, RUIN
rule (noun) see RULE (noun)
rule (verb) see RULE (verb)
run after see CHASE
rush see HURRY, RUSH, SPEED
ruthless see CRUEL

S

sad see SAD, UNHAPPY
safe see SAFE
salvage see RESCUE
same see EVEN, SAME
satisfied see CERTAIN, PROUD
satisfy see PLEASE
savage see FIERCE, VIOLENT
save see COLLECT, KEEP, RESCUE, SAVE
say see SAY
scalding see HOT
scamper see RUN
scare see FRIGHTEN, SCARE
scared see AFRAID
scene see VIEW
scent see SMELL
scoop see DIG
scorching see HOT
scoured see CLEAN
scowl see SULK
scramble see RUSH
scrap see PIECE
scream see SCREAM, YELL
screech see SCREAM, YELL
scribble see WRITE

scrumptious see DELICIOUS
scurry see HURRY
secret see SECRET
secrete see HIDE
secure see KNOT, SAFE
see see KNOW, SEE
seething see MAD
segment see PART, PIECE
seize see GRAB, TAKE
select see CHOOSE, PICK
self-centred see SELFISH
self-important see VAIN
selfish see GREEDY, MEAN (adj), SELFISH
send see SEND
sensible see SENSIBLE
serene see CALM, MILD, PEACEFUL
serious see SERIOUS
set see READY
set off see GO (verb)
set out see LEAVE
set up see START
settle see STAY
severe see STRICT
shade see COLOUR
shadowy see DARK
shake see SHAKE
shambles see MESS
share see SHARE
sharp see ALERT, SHARP
shatter see BREAK (verb)
shelter see PROTECT
shield see PROTECT
shine see SHINE
shiny see BRIGHT, SMOOTH
shiver see SHAKE
short see SHORT
shout see CALL, SHOUT
shove see PUSH
show off see BOAST
show see SHOW
shower see RAIN
shriek see SCREAM
shudder see SHAKE
shy see SHY
sick see ILL
side with see AGREE
significant see SPECIAL
signify see MEAN (verb)
silent see QUIET, SILENT
silly see SILLY
similar to see LIKE (adj)
simple see CLEAR, EASY, SIMPLE
sincere see REAL
skate see SLIDE
sketch see DRAW
skid see SLIDE
skilful see ABLE
skinny see THIN
slay see KILL
sleek see SMOOTH
sleep see REST, SLEEP
sleepy see TIRED

slender see NARROW, THIN
slice see CUT
slide see SLIDE
slim see NARROW, THIN
slip see SLIDE
slit see TEAR
sloppy see UNTIDY
slothful see LAZY
slow see SLOW
sluggish see SLOW
slumber see SLEEP
small see LITTLE, SHORT, SMALL, TINY
smart see BRIGHT, CLEVER
smear see MARK
smell see SMELL
smooth see EVEN, SMOOTH
smudge see MARK
snack see MEAL
snap see BREAK (verb)
snatch see GRAB
snooping see NOSY
snooze see SLEEP
snug see COSY, TIGHT
soaking see WET
soar see FLY
sob see MOAN
soggy see WET
soil see LAND (noun)
sole see ONLY (adj)
solemn see SERIOUS
solitary see ONLY (adj)
soothe see HEAL
sopping see WET
sore see PAINFUL
sorry see SORRY
sort see SORT
soundless see QUIET, SILENT
sour see BAD
spare see SPARE
sparkle see SHINE
speak see SPEAK, TALK,
special see SPECIAL
species see KIND (noun)
speed see SPEED
speedy see FAST
spin see SPIN, TURN
spiral see ROUND
spiteful see NASTY, UNKIND
splendid see GOOD
split see SHARE, TEAR
spoil see RUIN
spoiled see BAD
spot see FIND, MARK, NOTICE
spotless see CLEAN
spring see JUMP
sprint see RUN
spurn see REFUSE
squabble see ARGUE
squander see WASTE
squat see SHORT
stack see PILE
stain see MARK

standard see ORDINARY
star see ACTOR
stare at see WATCH
stare see LOOK
start see START
startle see FRIGHTEN, SCARE
starving see HUNGRY
state see SAY, TELL
stay see STAY
stern see STRICT
still see CALM
stinging see PAINFUL
stir see WAKE CHOOSE, GRAB, TAKE
stony see ROUGH
stop see END (verb), FINISH,
story see STORY
stout see STRONG
straightforward see CLEAR, EASY
strange see EXTRAORDINARY
strap see BAND
strict see STRICT
stride see WALK
strident see NOISY
strike see HIT
strip see BAND
strive see TRY
stroll see WALK
strong see STRONG
stronger see BETTER
struggle see FIGHT
stuff see FILL
stupid see STUPID
sturdy see STRONG, TOUGH
subject see MATTER
subsequent see NEXT
succeed see WIN
sudden see SUDDEN
sufficient see ENOUGH
suggestion see IDEA
sulk see SULK
super see GOOD
superb see EXCELLENT
superb see BETTER
support see HELP
sure see CERTAIN, SURE
surly see RUDE
surplus see REST
surprising see SUDDEN
suspect see DOUBT, GUESS
swallow see EAT
sway see WAVE
swell see GROW
sweltering see HOT
swift see FAST, QUICK
swoop see FLY

T

take see CARRY
take place see HAPPEN
tale see STORY
talk see SPEAK, TALK
tall see HIGH, TALL

tantrum see TEMPER
task see JOB
tasty see DELICIOUS
teacher see TEACHER
tear see TEAR
tease see ANNOY
tedious see BORING
tell see TALK, TELL
temper see TEMPER
tender see GENTLE
tepid see WARM
terrified see AFRAID
terrify see FRIGHTEN, SCARE
terror see FEAR
test see CHECK
thaw see MELT
theory see IDEA
thick see THICK
thin see NARROW, THIN
thing see OBJECT, THING
think see GUESS, THINK
thirsty see DRY
threat see DANGER
thrill see PLEASE
thrilled see EXCITED, HAPPY
thriving see WELL (adj)
throbbing see PAINFUL
throw away see WASTE
throw see THROW
thrust see PUSH
thump see HIT
thunderous see LOUD
tidy see NEAT, TIDY
tie see KNOT
tight see TIGHT
timid see NERVOUS, SHY
tint see COLOUR
tiny see LITTLE, SMALL, TINY
tip see TOP
tired see TIRED
toddler see BABY, CHILD
toil see WORK
top see TOP
topic see MATTER
toss see THROW
total (adj) see WHOLE
total (verb) see COUNT
totally see QUITE
touch down see LAND (verb)
touch see FEEL, TOUCH
tough see HARD, TOUGH, STRONG
tow see PULL
towering see HIGH, TALL
trace see DRAW, FIND
track see CHASE, FOLLOW
trail see FOLLOW
transfer see MOVE, PASS
transform see CHANGE
transmit see SEND
transparent see CLEAR
transport see CARRY
trap see CATCH, TRAP

travel *see* TRAVEL
treat *see* TREAT
trek *see* JOURNEY
tremble *see* SHAKE
trick *see* TRICK
trim *see* CUT, NEAT
trip *see* JOURNEY, VISIT (noun)
triumph *see* WIN
trouble *see* PROBLEM
true *see* REAL, TRUE
trust *see* TRUST
try *see* GO (noun), TRY
tubby *see* FAT
tug *see* PULL
tunnel *see* DIG
turn *see* BEND (verb), TURN (verb)
turn up *see* APPEAR
tutor *see* TEACHER
twirl *see* SPIN
twist *see* BEND (verb), WIND (verb)
type *see* KIND (noun), SORT

U

ugly *see* AWFUL, UGLY
unachievable *see* IMPOSSIBLE
unattractive *see* UGLY
unbelievable *see* INCREDIBLE
unbutton *see* UNDO
unclouded *see* CLEAR
uncork *see* OPEN (verb)
under *see* UNDER
underneath *see* UNDER
understand *see* KNOW, UNDERSTAND
undo *see* UNDO
undressed *see* BARE
unearth *see* DISCOVER
uneasy *see* NERVOUS
unexpected *see* SUDDEN
unfair *see* UNFAIR
unfasten *see* OPEN (verb)
unfreeze *see* MELT
unfriendly *see* MEAN
ungenerous *see* SELFISH
unhappy *see* SAD, UNHAPPY
unharmed *see* SAFE
uninteresting *see* BORING
unique *see* SPECIAL
unite *see* JOIN
unjust *see* UNFAIR
unkind *see* NASTY, UNKIND
unknown *see* SECRET
unlocked *see* OPEN (adj)
unoccupied *see* EMPTY, FREE
unpleasant *see* AWFUL, HORRIBLE
untamed *see* WILD
untidy *see* UNTIDY
untie *see* UNDO
unusual *see* EXTRAORDINARY, FUNNY, WEIRD
unwell *see* ILL
unwind *see* RELAX
unwise *see* SILLY

unwrap *see* OPEN (verb)
unyielding *see* HARD
upon *see* ABOVE
upset *see* SAD
urgent *see* IMPORTANT, URGENT
use *see* TREAT, USE
useful *see* USEFUL
useless *see* USELESS
usher *see* LEAD
utilize *see* USE
utter *see* SAY

V

vacant *see* EMPTY, FREE
vain *see* VAIN
value *see* RESPECT
vanish *see* VANISH
variety *see* KIND (noun)
vary *see* CHANGE
vast *see* BIG, GREAT, WIDE
very *see* VERY
vicious *see* CRUEL, FIERCE, NASTY
view *see* VIEW, WATCH
vigorous *see* ACTIVE
violent *see* VIOLENT
virtuous *see* GOOD
visit (noun) *see* VISIT
visit (verb) *see* CALL
visitor (noun) *see* VISITOR
vista *see* VIEW
voracious *see* GREEDY
voyage *see* JOURNEY

W

wail *see* MOAN
wait *see* WAIT
wake *see* WAKE
walk *see* WALK
want *see* MISS, NEED, WANT
wanted *see* WELCOME
warm *see* COSY, WARM
wash *see* WASH
washed *see* CLEAN
waste *see* RUBBISH, WASTE
watch *see* LOOK, WATCH
watchful *see* ALERT
wave *see* WAVE
way *see* WAY
weak *see* WEAK
wealth *see* TREASURE
wealthy *see* RICH
weary *see* TIRED
weighty *see* HEAVY
weird *see* ODD, STRANGE, WEIRD
welcome *see* WELCOME
well (adj) *see* BETTER, WELL (adj)
well (adv) *see* WELL (adv)
well-behaved *see* GOOD
well-kept *see* TIDY
well-known *see* FAMOUS
well-to-do *see* RICH
wet *see* WET

whine *see* MOAN
whirl *see* SPIN
whole *see* WHOLE
wicked *see* BAD, EVIL, WICKED
wide *see* THICK, WIDE
wield *see* USE
wild *see* WILD
win *see* WIN
wind *see* WIND
wise *see* SENSIBLE
wisecrack *see* JOKE
witness *see* SEE
wonderful *see* EXCELLENT
woods *see* WOODS
work *see* JOB, WORK
worn out *see* TIRED
worry *see* CARE, PROBLEM, WORRY
worship *see* ADMIRE, LOVE
worthless *see* USELESS
wound *see* HURT
wreck *see* DAMAGE, DESTROY, RUIN,
write *see* WRITE
wrong *see* EVIL, WRONG

Y

yell *see* CALL, SCREAM, SHOUT, YELL
young *see* YOUNG
youngster *see* CHILD
yummy *see* DELICIOUS

Z

zero *see* ZERO
zoom *see* SPEED